"Wayne Barkhuizen has produced a most helpful guide for anyone seeking more insight into the treasured story of Esther. This compact commentary is embedded with interesting nuggets while still keeping pace with the flow of the narrative. It's also a great reminder for someone like myself, with a Jewish/Gentile family background, of the rich heritage we have in a gracious God who has acted in history to save his people from bondage in Egypt, genocide in Persia and, ultimately, eternity in hell through the timely rescue of our crucified Messiah. This book will encourage you to rejoice and trust in the God who is always present, even when it seems like he is not!"

–Rt. Rev. Glenn Lyons, presiding bishop of REACH-SA

"Wayne Barkhuizen has done the Church of Christ worldwide a great favor with his book *God Behind the Scenes*. Here is an excellent presentation of the message of the book of Esther. Written simply and very engagingly, Wayne puts Esther in historical perspective and also succeeds in putting flesh and blood on all the characters in the story. This book is a great reminder of the providence and sovereignty of God over all of life and his special care for his own people.

Wayne reminds us that God's love, ultimately displayed through his Son our Lord Jesus on the cross, is shown in Esther to be constantly in action behind the scenes, even in the most precarious circumstances.

Wayne puts the reader in touch with the main themes of the book–complete with occasional historical references that are very helpful–then skilfully draws all these themes together at the end.

This is an altogether helpful book that will not only be a great help to individual Christians but also helpful for those who meet in group studies. I highly recommend it."

–Rt. Rev. Frank Retief,
former presiding bishop of REACH-SA

"The book of Esther poses numerous challenges for Christian readers. Barkhuizen helpfully guides us through the story to understand the God who, though never named, stands behind it and with his people. This guidance, along with theological reflections throughout, shows how and why this book remains important today."

—David Firth, author of *The Message of Esther*

"Wayne Barkhuizen has given us a fresh and insightful take on the book of Esther. ... [T]he author takes us through the book as Christian Scripture, deepening our appreciation of the magnificent providence of God at work in the history of the Jewish people. Simply written, this book will be a help to preachers, teachers, and general readers."

—Rev. Dr. David Seccombe, retired principal of George Whitefield College, South Africa

"I feel privileged to commend Wayne Barkhuizen's wonderful little book on a wonderful Old Testament story. If you want the book of Esther to light up, this is the way in for you. I can't think of a better one. And the message where God is seen working in a sovereign and hidden way in the darkest of times comes through with deep relevance for us in these present times of deep national, international, and personal stress and distress. Wayne shows how this little Old Testament book speaks with deep meaning directly into our own contemporary and troubled context. This volume also vividly illustrates how big dynamite can come in a small package. Read, study, put a bomb under your seat, and be inspired."

—Michael Cassidy, founder of African Enterprise, author of *The Church Jesus Prayed For*

"Wayne Barkhuizen has written a highly readable and insightful guide for individuals or groups studying the book of Esther. The reflection questions are sure to inspire some lively thought–and debate! I can recommend it highly to Bible readers who want to begin digging deeper into this fascinating narrative."

–Anthony Tomasino, author of *1 and 2 Kings, 1 and 2 Chronicles, Ezra, Nehemiah, Esther* (Zondervan Illustrated Bible Backgrounds Commentary) and *Evangelical Exegetical Commentary: Esther*

GOD BEHIND THE SCENES

THE BOOK OF ESTHER

Other titles in the Transformative Word series:

When You Want to Yell at God: The Book of Job
by Craig G. Bartholomew

Faith Amid the Ruins: The Book of Habakkuk
by Heath A. Thomas

Revealing the Heart of Prayer: The Gospel of Luke
By Craig G. Bartholomew

Together for the World: The Book of Acts
by Michael R. Wagenman

Cutting Ties with Darkness: 2 Corinthians
by John D. Barry

Between the Cross and the Throne: The Book of Revelation
by Matthew Y. Emerson

GOD BEHIND THE SCENES

THE BOOK OF ESTHER

TRANSFORMATIVE WORD

WAYNE K. BARKHUIZEN

Edited by Craig G. Bartholomew

God Behind the Scenes: The Book of Esther
Transformative Word

Lexham Press, 1313 Commercial St., Bellingham, WA 98225
LexhamPress.com

Print ISBN 9781577996590
Digital ISBN 9781577997122

Series Editor: Craig G. Bartholomew
Lexham Editorial Team: Lynnea Fraser, Abby Salinger, Claire Brubaker, Elizabeth Vince, Abigail Stocker
Cover Design: Christine Gerhart
Typesetting: ProjectLuz.com

TABLE OF CONTENTS

The lot is cast into the lap, but its
every decision is from the LORD.

Proverbs 16:33

1

INTRODUCTION

Everyone loves a good story. Stories are exciting and suspenseful, designed to captivate. The book of Esther is no exception. The iconic opening words of fairy tales (many of which convey truths about life, despite being make-believe), "Once upon a time, many years ago," would fit well in the Esther story. But Esther isn't merely a story designed to entertain or convey truth, and it isn't even simply a means of retelling history so that it won't be forgotten—though it accomplishes all of these things. Rather, Esther is a story that chronicles God's surprising preservation of his people when their very existence is threatened by a superpower.

Even more important, the Esther story chronicles how God fulfills his purposes to ultimately bring salvation to the world through a Jewish descendant (Gen 3:15; 12:2–3; 2 Sam 7:16). For if all the Jews throughout the entire Persian Empire had been annihilated, God would not have been able to fulfill his promise. This is why Esther is such a memorable story—one etched into history and one from which we can learn.[1]

A Strange Absence

Throughout the book of Esther God appears to be glaringly absent; he isn't named or mentioned. In fact, he is conspicuous by his absence![2] But as the story unfolds, with all its unexpected twists and turns, we as readers are confronted with events that unmistakably point to God's invisible presence throughout. After all, who else is capable of orchestrating such remarkable—and even unbelievable—twists and turns that always favor the preservation of God's people, the Jews? The only logical conclusion is that God is profoundly present even when he appears to be absent. This is reassuring and comforting for God's people of all ages: He is always present and never absent, even when his presence isn't obvious.

> God is profoundly present—even when he appears to be absent.

Overview

The entire story of Esther is set outside Israel in the Persian city of Susa (alternately spelled Suza).[3] Years earlier God's people had been banished from their homeland—this banishment was God's judgment for their disobedience. Although they had since been allowed to return, many Jews like Mordecai and Esther had elected to remain living under foreign rulers away from their homeland. The book of Esther thus provides insight into the fortunes of the Jews who never returned to the promised land after the exile had ended.

Esther is the story of how some of the descendants of Abraham, the Jews, faced the threat of annihilation under the Persian superpower, and how God rescued them from destruction. Instead of being obliterated, the Jews were delivered and then empowered, as agents of God's judgment, to destroy their enemies.

OUTLINE OF THE BOOK OF ESTHER

Scene One: A Pretty Jew in the King's Palace (Esth 1:1–2:18)

Scene Two: A Jewish Holocaust Looms (Esth 2:19–3:15)

Scene Three: A Jewish Queen to the Rescue (Esth 4:1–5:8)

Scene Four: A Jew Honored by His Archenemy (Esth 5:9–6:14)

Scene Five: An End to the Enemy of the Jews (Esth 7:1–10)

Scene Six: A Royal Edict Saves the Jews (Esth 8:1–10:3)

The Theological Center of Esther

Although the book of Esther is unique in that it contains no references to God, specific developments throughout the story and in the way the narrator tells it indicate that God, the invisible presence, is the mastermind behind all that occurs.[4] For example, when Queen Esther's cousin Mordecai calls her to risk her own life, he concludes, "Who knows but that you have come to your royal position for such a time as this?" (Esth 4:14). With this statement Mordecai implies that Esther's presence in the palace is God's means of saving her people: She is to use her strategic royal position to be the instrument of rescue so that God's purposes will not be thwarted but fulfilled. Esther is therefore portrayed as a savior figure—just as God had used others throughout history for that purpose.

Origin of the Title

The title of the book is taken from the name of one of the story's main characters, Esther. This is one of only two Bible books named after a woman. Ruth, the Moabite, also has a book named after her. Other books in the Bible contain references to prominent women who played significant roles in Israel's history, such as the judge Deborah. So Esther finds herself in the rather illustrious company of select women who played an especially important role in the life of God's people, the Jews, in the grand story of Scripture.

The Story's Hero/Heroine

Although the book is named after Esther, who is indeed one of the dominant characters of the story, in the end it is Mordecai—not Esther—who is hailed for his greatness (Esth 10). The storyteller doesn't portray Esther as the heroine as much as he portrays Mordecai as the hero. This raises the question of why the storyteller didn't name the book after Mordecai. In this detail the writer was no doubt making a subtle point for his readers to uncover. However, Jewish commentator Adele Berlin cautions us against assigning the title "hero" to just one character:

> It is difficult to choose one hero because Esther and Mordecai share this role. The two work as a team, one initially from inside the palace and the other from the outside, and then at the end, when both are at the heart of the government, they wield their authority in concert. To the extent that the plot revolves around the rivalry and enmity between Haman and Mordecai, Mordecai is the hero. However, it is in fact Esther who plans and carries out the actions that save the Jews, making her the true hero.[5]

Is the real hero of the story left unnamed?

SUGGESTED READING

- ☐ Read the whole book of Esther to familiarize yourself with the story.

Reflection

How does Esther's divinely appointed position in the palace reassure you that God played an active part in her story and continues to play an active role in your own?

____

____

____

____

What effect does the lack of reference to God in the Esther story create in your mind?

____

____

____

____

Who, in your opinion, is the hero of the Esther story? Why?

____

____

____

____

2

A PORTRAIT OF ESTHER

The book of Esther is a story of Jews facing the threat of annihilation while living far away from their homeland, and of how God used Esther and Mordecai to save them. The story ends with these Jews celebrating the feast of Purim to remember the events recounted in the book.

The Jewish Feast of Purim

Purim—ironically named after the lot that the story's villain cast to determine the date when the Jews would meet their end (Esth 3:7)—is celebrated as a memorial feast at the end of the Esther story. The story of Esther concludes not just with the institution of the feast of Purim but also with instructions for the celebration of this feast in perpetuity. This ensures that Jews from generation to generation will remember how God rescued their ancestors from the nearly catastrophic events that threatened their very existence.

Jews still celebrate this festival annually. Patricia Tull explains, "During this festival, the book is read aloud. Participants dress up as characters from the book and a carnival atmosphere reigns. Food and drink are given as gifts and charity is given to the poor."[1] Performing skits depicting the events are another way people interact with the story.[2]

Historical Background

The events recorded in the Esther story occur during an epoch of history in which Persia was the dominant world superpower (550–330 BC).[3] The Persian king Xerxes, who ruled from 486–465 BC, was a mighty, powerful figure who was accustomed to doing whatever he pleased.

RULERS OF THE PERSIAN (ACHAEMENID) EMPIRE

Ruler	Reign (approximate dates)
Darius I (the Great)	522–486 BC
Xerxes I (Ahasuerus)	**486–465 BC**
Artaxerxes I	464–424 BC
Xerxes II	424–423 BC
Darius II	423–404 BC

Because of this, he comes into sharp conflict with the real superpower of the universe, who is orchestrating outcomes behind the scenes in the Esther story. The situation is reminiscent of Psalm 2, which describes the world rulers as waging war against God, only to discover that he is not going to capitulate to their puny powers—considerable though they may be from a human perspective. He alone is God Almighty, and there really isn't any contest in this power struggle. This is evidenced throughout the Bible as God again and again proves himself invincible. No rival superpowers on earth will be able to thwart God's purposes—ever!

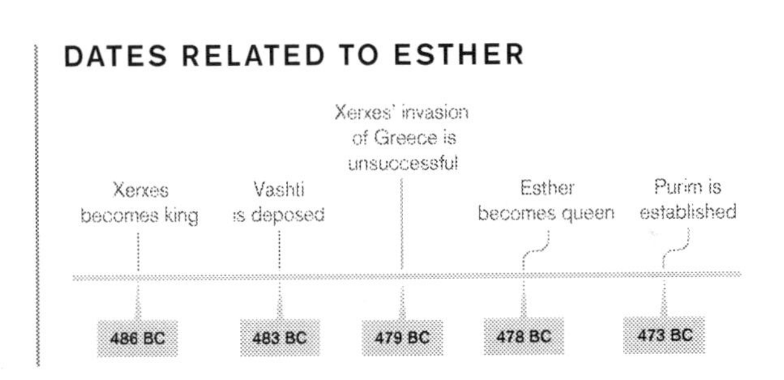

While this power play goes on in Persia, the Persian king and his people are oblivious to God's grand purposes for his people. This reality prefigures the ultimate salvation God would accomplish for the world in the arrival of his king, Jesus (Matt 1:21).

An "Exiled" Jewish Nation—under Foreign Rule

God's people's lingering presence in Persia at this time in history raises several questions. Why did a number of them not return to the promised land after the end of the exile, as God's prophets had urged them to do? Was it wrong for these Jewish exiles to continue to enjoy the prosperity of life under the rule of the superpower of the day in the Persian capital city, Susa, and elsewhere in the empire? Was this new threat to their very existence from the nation in which they sought shelter and security not a reason for them to leave now? Yet God in his grace had not abandoned or forgotten them.

GOD'S SUPREMACY

The encounters that God's people, the descendants of Abraham, have had with world superpowers throughout history have always proven God's supremacy—whether the situation be the face-off between Moses and the Egyptian pharaoh (Exod 6:28–7:5) or that between Daniel and the Babylonian king (Dan 3:1–23). But he doesn't always save in the ways we would expect or hope, as was the case with Jesus who wasn't spared from crucifixion and tragically also the Jews during the Holocaust. However, all such atrocities will be judged by God with absolute justice. The book of Revelation also declares that at the very end of history God alone will rule, and that he will reign forever and ever. He is the uncontested ruler of the universe he created; he alone has the sovereign right to rule.

Previously God had threatened that if his people were to rebel against him they would face his unavoidable judgment. This had already occurred in the exile, when the Jewish homeland was vacated by its people—and this had been God's doing! (The northern kingdom had been exiled earlier, in 722 BC; the destruction and exile of the southern kingdom had taken place in 587/6 BC). However, after they had served the sentence of God's heavy hand of judgment against them in exile, surely the right thing for God's people would be to return to the land of promise. Yet some of God's people remained in exile even after his chastisement of them was over (Jer 29:10; Ezek 37:12–14).

Esther and Mordecai's lack of distinctiveness as Jews in the initial stages of the story seems to indicate that, rather than opting to retain their unique, God-prescribed identity, they had blended into the Persian culture. Nevertheless, they were Jewish by birth, and this plays a major role in the story. The Persians possessed the political will and power to exterminate the Jews, which would have severely compromised God's plan of salvation for the whole world. All Jews everywhere in the Persian Empire would have been at risk.

THE PERSIAN EMPIRE

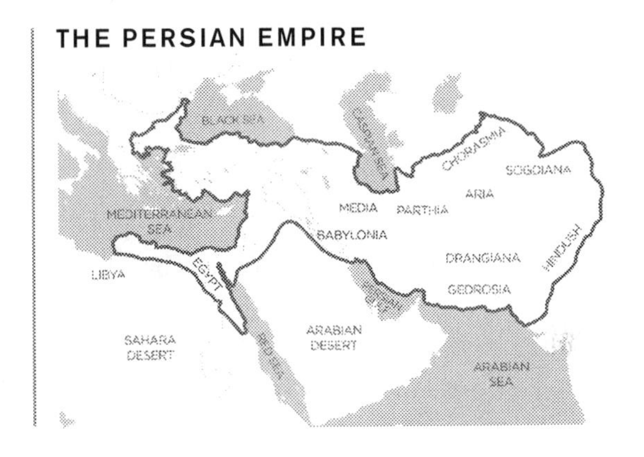

That the Persian ruler, King Xerxes, was powerful enough to annihilate these Jews played right into the hands of the story's villain, Haman, who abused his relationship with the king to try to settle a personal grudge against a specific Jew, Mordecai. Haman went for broke to eliminate the Jews. Yet he did not count on the invisible presence of God, the most powerful ruler of all, who thwarted his dastardly plot to ethnically cleanse the empire of Jews and to promote his personal ambition for power. Haman's increasingly apparent ambition is just one of the political power plays throughout the story.

A Profound Message

The story of Esther demonstrates that God will not be inactive in a world that is hostile to him and his people. He would rescue the Jews from genocide to ensure that a future Jewish descendant, a son of Abraham (Matt 1:17), would be born to deliver his people from death and destruction. The message of Esther is a special reminder to God's "exiled" people that he has not forgotten or abandoned them—and that he never will. So even though at times in the narrative God appears to have gone missing, he is actually profoundly present. He may be unseen, but he is unmistakably there.

The message of Esther is a special reminder to God's "exiled" people that he has not forgotten or abandoned them—and that he never will.

Our position on this side of the cross likewise reminds us that we, as Christians, like these Jews in a foreign land, are not at home. We too still live as exiles (1 Pet 2:11), and we too can be sure of God's presence both now and forever.

SUGGESTED READING

- ☐ Psalm 2:1–12
- ☐ 1 Peter 2:9–13

Reflection

What events in the world today make you wonder whether God is actually present? How does the story of Esther challenge these feelings?

____

____

____

____

The celebration of the feast of Purim reminds the Jews of their deliverance from annihilation; how can you, as a Christian, remember God's deliverance?

____

____

____

____

Do you ever get the feeling that God may have abandoned you? How can the Esther story help you combat this sentiment?

____

____

____

____

3

NARRATIVE: THE FASCINATION OF STORY

The Bible is God's story. Our task is to find out where both the Jews in Esther's time and we ourselves in our day fit into this story.

The grand story of the Bible begins with God creating people to be in a loving relationship with himself. His desire was to be their God and for them to be his people (Exod 6:7; Jer 7:23; Ezek 36:28). However, our first ancestors rebelled against God's loving rule and so forfeited that perfect relationship. Subsequently they were banished from God's presence. But God promised a rescuer (Gen 3:15) and later started afresh with one man, Abraham. God promised to bless him and to give him many descendants, as well as a land in which to live as an inheritance (Gen 12:1–3). God also promised the nation composed of Abraham's descendants that a descendant of King David would rule forever (2 Sam 7:14). However, once again God's people rebelled against him; the consequence this time was banishment from the land of promise. But God promised that this exile would end (Jer 30:3), and this promise was fulfilled under the reign of King Cyrus, the Persian ruler who permitted the Jewish exiles to return to their land in 539 BC. Around this time he conquered the Babylonians, and the Assyrians—who had originally exiled the northern kingdom of Israel—also came under his control.[1]

BABYLONIAN AND ASSYRIAN EXILES

This is the time frame in which our story of Esther takes place. While some Jewish exiles had returned to the promised land, many had not—including Esther, Mordecai, and many others living in the Persian capital city of Susa. Little did they recognize the grave danger lurking in Susa that would threaten their very existence. The king under whose authority they were living was, after all, a Persian—not a Jewish—king.

Literary Background

Authorship and Date

There is no indication of who wrote the book of Esther; no clues are given in the book to help us determine the identity of the author or authors. But whoever wrote it was familiar with life in Persia, suggesting that the author was most likely either a Jew living in exile some time after these events had transpired or someone who had researched these details thoroughly enough to record the story with accuracy. Some suggest that Mordecai himself was the author, but there are no hints in the book to substantiate this.

Likewise, there is no clarity about when the book of Esther was written. The story was most likely recorded in the fourth, or possibly the third century BC.[2] This would ensure that the feast of Purim would be celebrated for all time among the Jews. Amélie Kuhrt asserts that the book of Esther "was almost certainly written in the Hellenistic period."[3]

Literary Contours

Storytelling is a powerful means of communication. After all, stories are easy to remember, and they're easy to tell to others. Using story to record history ensures that history will be passed on from one generation to the next. The Esther account is brilliantly crafted and communicates the gripping story of God's rescue of the Jewish people as they faced certain destruction. But we don't get the full message of Esther from reading just a snippet of the text.[4]

As readers of this story, we should bear in mind that a storyteller always has a perspective on events that will shape the narrative, even if the storyteller was not present when the events transpired. In this regard, Meir Steinberg ascribes omniscience to the biblical narrator, an attribution that reflects God's omniscience.[5] The biblical narrator has inside information about private conversations, as well as about the characters' thoughts and feelings, although he doesn't always choose to disclose them.

Readers of stories also need to understand what the storyteller intends to communicate in the narrative—whether that intention is stated or (as is most often the case) unstated, as in Esther. As with most stories, the narrative of Esther doesn't provide all of the background information or full details. Such omissions often result in gaps—discontinuities that readers need to fill in for themselves as they read and reread the story, searching for clues.

The gaps in the narrative invite readers to engage with the story, to make assumptions regarding the storyteller's intent when he does not reveal it. Details given in the story can inform our conclusions, as can familiarity with the background of the original intended audience. Sternberg remarks on the effects these gaps in a story create for us as readers:

> Among these functions of ambiguity, the most basic consist in the manipulation of narrative interest: curiosity, suspense, surprise. The withholding of information about the past, especially if it deforms the plot line—the effect appearing before or without cause—at once stimulates the reader's *curiosity* about the action, the agents, their life and relations below the surface, the world they inhabit. To make sense of them, [the reader] will try to resolve the gaps; failing that, he will look forward to new disclosures; so that a gradual release

> of clues will keep him happily busy on the horns of ambiguity.[6]

The Esther story is written about the Jews in "exile," whose Jewishness, as well as their knowledge of Scripture, must have shaped their interpretation of the events they were experiencing. A Jew reading Esther and discovering that God is not mentioned in the story has to fill in the gaps to conclude that God really is present even though he is not referenced or acknowledged. Another such gap was created when the storyteller chose not to disclose the reason for Queen Vashti's revolt; this may generate sympathy for her in readers' minds, as she comes across as a courageous woman struggling to survive in a man's world.

The Use of Satire, Humor, and Irony

The author of Esther uses satire and irony throughout the story.[7] Various scenes are understatedly humorous. This is a type of poetic irony—tragic events depicted in ways that resemble comedy. As you read, you may find yourself chuckling at events that occur in the most unexpected fashion. The sequence in chapter 6 is particularly comical. Esther's original Jewish audience would certainly have delighted in seeing Haman—contrary to his expectations and ambitions—fail to receive what he thought he deserved and instead having to endure what he hated, while facing humiliation in the process. This antagonist was the Jews' enemy, and his demise was beneficial for the survival of the Jews.

Berlin likewise notes that "the Book of Esther is the most humorous of the books in the Bible, amusing throughout and at certain points uproariously funny."[8] Irony plays a big part in the story. Many incidents of reversals of fortune in it prove ironic. For example, Haman craves honor, yet Mordecai is honored instead. And Haman constructs a capital punishment device on which to execute his archenemy, then ironically ends up being hanged on it.

Building the Plot

The Esther story, like most stories, starts with an introduction, proceeds to the main body of the narrative, and then ends with a conclusion. David Beldman succinctly explains the stages of a basic narrative: "A basic plot line unfolds along the lines of (1) exposition, (2) complication, (3) change, (4) unraveling, and (5) ending."[9] The Esther story fits this pattern. As it unfolds, the tension builds. It starts with a spectacular banquet, which takes a sudden twist with the unexpected defiance of the queen when summoned by the king. Her absence opens the door for Esther, who eventually secures the salvation of the Jews.

Many details in Esther that appear to be incidental later prove significant—like the recording of current history in the king's annals. The king's discovery from these annals that Mordecai hasn't received credit for exposing a murderous plot against him leads to him belatedly honoring Mordecai. And then there are mundane bits of information—like the king's sleeplessness—that profoundly shape the outcome of the story, reversing the fortunes of the Jews. Can it be possible that this seemingly insignificant factor can turn the tide of destruction?

The queen approaching the king—at risk of death—leaves us feeling anxious about the outcome: Will she live or die? Likewise, in the larger scheme of things, will the threatened Jewish minority survive in Persia, where the powerful second-in-command is hostile to their very existence? If so, who will come to their rescue? This evil villain schemes to wipe out all of the Jews, but will he get his way? He initially appears to succeed; everything seems to be proceeding according to plan. But the deferred reward the king pronounces, at the least opportune moment for the villain, results in the rise of the villain's nemesis and his own unexpected demise! Then Queen Esther masterfully orchestrates an exclusive feast with the king and his prime minister to uncover the murderous plot, which is the beginning of the villain's end and the consequent salvation of the Jews. And finally, when the king realizes the impending disaster that awaits these Jews—including his beloved queen—he is powerless to openly spare their lives, for the edict he himself has allowed to be put into effect cannot be rescinded. Will these Jews survive the threat of genocide? As in all good stories, the ending is happy: The villain is eliminated, and the good guy emerges victorious.

The tempo quickens as the story progresses, resulting in an ever-mounting tension. The storyteller systematically doles out bits of information that will become significant in the next scene; this makes the story intriguing and fills in some of the gaps. For example, Mordecai exposes a conspiracy, and the incident is recorded in the king's annals (Esth 2:23); this loyal deed will be rewarded only when the king reads his annals when he cannot sleep (Esth 6:1).

Beldman reminds us that "attention to the plot helps to focus the theme and purpose of a narrative. … Old Testament plot renders to us the character of the God who addresses us: not distant or detached, but immersed in the life of Israel and also in our lives."[10] So as we read the story, fill in its gaps, and listen to its message, we hear God speaking to us too. He assures us that he is continually present in our own circumstances.

Although, as we have noted, the storyteller has inside information on private conversations and unspoken thoughts, he deliberately refrains from revealing the thoughts and motives of the characters; instead—and most effectively—he simply tells the story. David Firth insightfully points out that because Esther is a story and is narrated as such, this is key to interpreting it. In his words:

> Although it makes historical reference, its focus on storytelling requires us to consider this when interpreting it. This focus causes us to look at both the characters and the plot, though the deliberate decision not to tell us what motivates the characters invites us to explore their motives through the story's telling.[11]

Further, this also makes sense of God's absence; his presence is to be assumed by the Jewish reader and by us—even though the characters in the story seem oblivious to God's guidance.

Historical Narrative

There is considerable debate concerning the historicity of the Esther narrative: Is it fact or fiction? We can find arguments for both positions.[12] Berlin wades into the matter of its historicity, saying:

> To the ancient reader an imaginative story was just as worthy, or even as holy, as a historically accurate one, so to declare Esther to be imaginative does not in any way detract from its value. The message of the Book of Esther and the significance of Purim remain the same whether or not the events of the book were actual.[13]

The storyteller may have even taken poetic license to assign fictional names to the characters in the story to represent actual people in history; these wordplays are then lost in translation.[14] There are difficulties, for example, in substantiating the names of the characters from the historical records of that period, and there are no known records to verify that the law of the Medes and the Persians was unchangeable (though this point comes up in the Daniel story as well).

The storyteller, however, intended the Esther story to be read as history (Esth 2:23; 10:2). Timothy Laniak comments:

> [It] seems inadvisable to disregard both the author's intentions and these historical details that speak together of actual events in

> the ancient world. Esther is not "history" as moderns would conceive of it. It is a great story with many traditional features, and it deserves merit as a historical source written close in time and space to the events it describes.[15]

The existence of the Feast of Purim and its celebration by the Jews places the story in history and serves as its historical basis.

> **THE LAWS**
>
> Every law issued by the king of the Medes and Persians is irrevocable and therefore unable to be retracted; the only way to override it is to issue a counter law. However, the words used to describe this unchangeable law could also mean that when such a law is issued, it could not be disobeyed or disregarded. But the unchangeable nature of any such law cannot be confirmed anywhere in Greek or Persian sources.[16]

Conveying Truth

The story of Esther conveys truth in a narrative format that tells the story of the preservation of God's people under threat of annihilation. At every point in the story God works behind the scenes, orchestrating events. He is the unnamed, unsung main character. And his involvement in the lives of his people still

The story of Esther conveys truth in a narrative format that tells the story of the preservation of God's people when under threat of annihilation.

living in "exile" in the city of Susa is a graphic reminder that he is present everywhere, working out his purposes according to his divine plans. For a more recent example, in South Africa, where I live, most of us recognize God's hidden hand at work in Nelson Mandela's release as a political prisoner to lead our country as president through a bloodless transition to democracy.

SUGGESTED READING

- ☐ Reread the whole Esther story.
- ☐ Isaiah 45
- ☐ Jeremiah 30–31
- ☐ Daniel 6

Reflection

What dramatic effect does the storyteller create by leaving gaps and opting not to disclose particular details in the story?

Do you think the Esther story is historical? What difference does it make if it is an imaginative story set in a historical context?

How does thinking of Esther as simply an intriguing story written to convey a message make it meaningful to you as a reader?

4

SCENE ONE: A PRETTY JEW IN THE PALACE OF A FOREIGN KING

We can derive great comfort from knowing that, even though it may not always appear as such, God reigns over all of human history. He has the ability to shift people into position to suit his purposes.

A Powerful Persian King Rules the World (Esther 1:1—2:1)

The storyteller begins by introducing us to a powerful Persian king,[1] who ruled his vast empire from his palace in the capital city of Susa.[2] The events of the Esther story unfold in this city. King Xerxes ruled an empire that spanned most of the then-known world.[3] Persia was a very powerful nation.[4]

The Esther story kicks off with an extravagant feast hosted by King Xerxes in the third year of his reign. All the nobles, officials, princes, and military leaders of his mighty army are invited (Esth 1:3). This feast was most likely designed to get everyone in the empire on board with King Xerxes' imminent assault against the Greeks.[5] This feast was impressive—supposedly lasting for six months. One of its main purposes was to flaunt Xerxes' wealth and royal majesty (Esth 1:4), and everybody would have been suitably impressed. By beginning the story with a description of this feast, the storyteller portrays the king as a seemingly invincible world ruler.

After the first feast, the king hosts yet another for the people living within the citadel (the palace grounds) of the city (Esth 1:5). This was probably in appreciation for their six months of hard work at the first feast. The storyteller goes into great detail concerning the ostentatious setting, honing in on the individualized wine goblets (Esth 1:6–7) with the apparent intention of showcasing the king's opulent wealth. At this banquet the king issues a command (Esth 1:8) instructing the royal attendants to let everyone drink as much as they please. This particular command implies extravagance and overconsumption—with its predictably associated drunkenness, although the story is inconclusive in this regard. Berlin writes that "the chapter reeks of drunken indulgence, royal incompetence, and sexual innuendo."[6] Jobes offers interesting insight on ancient customs, as revealed by Herodotus: "The ancients believed intoxication put them in closer touch with the spiritual world ... excessive drinking would have been an essential element of Xerxes' war council."[7] If this were the case, the description of this feast subtly introduces the duel of the gods—a theme that will implicitly play out throughout the story. Amélie Kuhrt insightfully observes that "at the centre of the imperial system was the Persian king. The great god Ahuramazda had set him over the varied lands and peoples of the earth and given Persia supremacy over them; without his divine support no king ruled Persia."[8]

At the end of the feast, when the king has imbibed too much wine, he decides to parade his beautiful queen before all of his distinguished guests (Esth 1:10–11). He wants to prove that his queen is the loveliest woman of all. He has already displayed his decadent wealth; now he wishes to make a statement about his queen's extraordinary beauty. It is at this early point that the story takes its first unexpected turn.

Queen Vashti Defies the King (Esther 1:12)

Vashti's refusal to obey the king's summons comes as a great surprise. No one has ever before dared to defy the all-powerful command of the Persian king. Unsurprisingly, he reacts in anger (Esth 1:12), humiliated by his wife's public defiance. He decides to consult with his advisers (Esth 1:13–15). This should not necessarily be interpreted as a sign of his weakness as king; rather, he is complying with Persian legal customs.

The storyteller suggests no reason for Queen Vashti's refusal to obey the king's summons; as readers, we are left to fill in the gap as to why she chooses to defy him and whether her action is justifiable. Some have suggested that she deemed it inappropriate to associate with men drinking at the feast, as she had been hosting a separate feast for the women. Another possible explanation is that the king had requested for her to appear naked—wearing only her royal crown. This seems unlikely. It is more likely that her declining to appear before the king constituted a refusal to humiliate herself to the level of a dancing girl before inebriated men.[9] However, the storyteller leaves us to ponder and make conjectures—and in so doing to become engaged with the story.

Regardless of Vashti's motivation, her refusal sets in motion a chain reaction that will be to the benefit of the Jews in the days to come. Is this merely coincidental, or is the suggestion already made that God is at work behind the scenes?

Queen Vashti Is Dethroned (Esther 1:13–17)

The king's advisers act to preserve their monarch's honor. The text describes them as men "who knew the times" (Esth 1:13 ESV), and Jobes notes that "they used astrology and other forms of divination to discern the propitious course of action."[10] Once again we are alerted to the battle that rages in the invisible realm. These royal experts conclude that Queen

Vashti's defiance may incite a revolt by the women in the empire—a potentiality that must be prevented (Esth 1:16–18). Queen Vashti must be stripped of her royal position immediately (Esth 1:19). Considering the events that unfold later in the story, it is rather surprising that Vashti does not lose her life for her defiance of the king's request.

This unexpected turn of events opens the door for another queen to be crowned—someone deemed "better" (Esth 1:19). Ironically, that probably refers to someone who is not defiant toward the king and his supreme authority.

King Xerxes Issues an Edict to Combat Defiance (Esther 1:18–22)

To prevent chaos from breaking out in his empire, where rightful authority (in this case, that of husbands over wives) is at risk, the king issues yet another command (Esth 1:21–22). Is the storyteller poking fun at the king here? Does the king really think this directive will prevent further defiance? But this seemingly minor detail about the law will take on great significance later in the story, for the law of the Medes and Persians cannot be changed![11] This edict is publicized to everyone in their own language so all people will be aware of the king's command (Esth 1:22). This is a distinct feature of the king's rule: He rules his kingdom by top-down directives.

On this note chapter 1 ends. In the first verse of chapter 2 we learn that the king still has a soft spot for the queen he has dethroned (Esth 2:1). There is just a hint here that, as he reflects soberly on his impulsiveness, he nurses regrets.[12] Ironically, he is trapped by his own law—the law of the Medes and the Persians, which cannot be repealed. This will not be the last time this snag will come into play. Regardless of the king's feelings for her, Vashti's fate is sealed; he cannot reverse his decision. The next logical course of action is to find a new queen—one who is better than Vashti; by contrast, Esther was compliant rather than defiant. So the search begins (Esth 2:2–4).

A Powerless Jew Finds Favor (Esther 2:2–18)

Esther has her audience with the king in the seventh year of his reign (Esth 2:16). Four years have passed since the feast at which Queen Vashti was deposed. The king's aides now make a proposal (Esth 2:2–4), which he accepts, and the search is on for a new queen.

King Xerxes Issues an Edict to Find a Queen (Esther 2:2–8)

The storyteller masterfully introduces us to one of the main characters in the story, Mordecai (Esth 2:5–6). The writer unapologetically identifies him as a Jew—an identification he will reiterate throughout the story whenever he mentions his name. The narrator reveals Mordecai's ancestry by tracing his family tree all the way back to a king of Israel, Saul, who ironically was less than exemplary (see 1 Sam 13:7–14). Even though it may appear irrelevant at this point, this ancestry will have significance as the story unfolds.

Another vital piece of information the author reveals is that Mordecai is living in "exile" in Persia as a Jew.[13] This is the reason for the Esther story: to remind the Jews that God is not interested merely in those Jews who have returned to their promised homeland but also in those who have elected for whatever reason not to uproot themselves—like Mordecai and Esther.

The storyteller then reveals Mordecai's relationship to Esther. She goes by two names: Hadassah, which means "myrtle" and is her Jewish name, and Esther, her Persian name (Esth 2:7). Esther happens to be an unusually attractive girl—in fact, she is stunning! But she has a sad background: Her parents have died, and Mordecai, her cousin, has adopted her as his own. This implies that, despite her phenomenal beauty, she has no status or position of influence.

The king, who does not take kindly to his commands being disobeyed, issues another edict—this time to recruit all of the prettiest girls in his empire as prospective candidates for queen (Esth 2:8). Esther, who lives in Susa, is "taken" (Esth 2:8). This implies that, in all likelihood, she has no say in the matter. She fits the criteria of the king's edict, so she is grabbed and placed in the king's harem with many other attractive girls, one of whom will be appointed queen to replace Vashti. Knowing her background, we can't help but wonder whether Esther stands any realistic chance of being crowned as the Persian queen. Once again God's invisible presence can be detected in the shadows, but there is no hint as to why Esther might be the most suitable replacement for Vashti.[14]

Esther Is Taken as a Prospective Queen (Esther 2:9–16)

The first big breakthrough is that Esther finds favor with Hegai, the man in charge of the king's harem (Esth 2:9). That she "pleased him and won his favor" probably refers to her exceptional natural beauty and charm. This is once again evidence of God's unseen hand at work, making sure that she is preferred over all the others and so positioning her on the inside track in the quest to be crowned queen. When her turn finally comes to impress the king, Esther listens to Hegai (Esth 2:15). She is his favorite, but will she go on to become the king's choice?

Take note of how the process worked: "In the evening she would go in, and in the morning she would return to the second harem in custody of Shaashgaz, the king's eunuch, who was in charge of the concubines" (Esth 2:14). Esther will have a "legal" one-night stand with the king, where she will have to impress him with her appearance as well as with her sexual prowess. If she makes a positive impression, she may be "summoned by name" (Esth 2:14 ESV) by the king to return to his presence. Esther's going to the king reflects poorly on her sexual purity and faithfulness to God (Exod 20:14; Judg 14:3), for the action clearly involves a compromise of her Jewish distinctiveness. She is not portrayed as a paragon of virtue, willing as she is to compromise her Jewish faith by sleeping with the pagan king—not that she has much choice, we realize. Still, she is not without options, though the consequences of being uncooperative would no doubt carry little prospect of a happy ending! Esther is not faithful as a Jew, but she is not faithless either; she has a Jewish heritage and would have been schooled in the Jewish Scriptures. Though these factors may appear latent now, later in the story they become significant when she discloses her Jewish identity.

The biggest surprise is Mordecai's instruction to Esther not to reveal her Jewish identity (Esth 2:10).

This enables her to remain undetected as a Jew until the appointed time for her to disclose her hidden identity. By that stage she would be the queen. His instruction subtly hints that some animosity may have existed toward the Jewish "exiles" living in Persia; we'll soon see that there certainly is a man in Persia who harbors a grudge against Jews.

Esther Is Enthroned as Queen (Esther 2:17–18)

Against all odds, Esther finds favor with the king and is enthroned as his new queen. To celebrate her royal appointment the king hosts a feast in her honor.[15] The earlier banquet in this story has ended badly, so what can be expected at this one?

We might ask why Esther wins the king's favor? It seems it is because of her stunning beauty (Esth 1:7) but also their sexual relationship[16] established in her one night with him.[17] The result is that she becomes an "undercover" Jewish queen in the Persian palace. Might there be an unmentioned explanation for her unexpected appointment? Surely this is not simply a convenient coincidence!

This ends the first scene of the story.

God at Work Behind the Scenes

Just as some of God's people were living in exile in Esther's time, we too still live in exile, for we are not at home yet in the new heavens and the new earth. First Peter 2:11 reminds scattered Christians to live as aliens and strangers in this world. The implication is that we are not to grow overly attached to this world and all it offers or to seek to blend in with the environment in which we find ourselves (1 John 2:15–17);

rather, we're to live to please God, realizing that God can use us—faults and all—for his purposes.

Our assurance is the sure knowledge that God can direct life's circumstances and events. He places us where we are to serve his purposes. He is moving all of history to its culmination—to the time when Jesus will return to rule forever.

The Esther story further reminds us that there is no need for us to be intimidated by powerful world rulers or their gods. They and their limitations are no match for God, who will reign forever as the unrivaled ruler of all (Rev 11:15). This reminds us where the real power lies—even if it is unseen.

God places us where we are to serve his purposes. He is moving all of history toward its culmination—the day when Jesus returns to rule forever.

SUGGESTED READING

- ☐ Esther 1:1–2:18
- ☐ Proverbs 21:1; 31:30
- ☐ Galatians 4:4
- ☐ 1 John 2:15–17

Reflection

How has the Esther story helped you see that God is at work behind the scenes, moving people into strategic places and positions at just the right time (Gal 4:4)?

Although the story's focus at this point is clearly on the invincible power of the king, how does it show that world rulers are not all that unshakable after all (Psa 2; Prov 21:1)?

The king is obsessed with beauty, wealth, and power. How should you, as a Christian, think about beauty in a world of power and wealth (Prov 31:30), especially if you are a woman?

5

SCENE TWO: A JEWISH HOLOCAUST LOOMS

Our enemy desires to destroy both human lives and all vestiges of faith in Jesus Christ (John 10:10). So while events in life may appear to be spiraling out of control, with hostile attacks that produce untold suffering being unleashed against God's people, we are to take comfort in the reality that God is anything but unaware of or unable to ward off these threats. This next scene serves as a reminder of this truth. Here, lovely Esther is crowned queen and finds herself in the king's palace. The storyteller then shifts the focus to Mordecai as a tense standoff occurs between him and Haman.

A Jew Saves the King from Death (Esther 2:19–23)

The storyteller describes Mordecai as "sitting at the king's gate" (Esth 2:19); this probably indicates that Mordecai holds a position in the royal civil service,[1] which enables him to have frequent access to Esther within the palace precincts.

Queen Esther's Identity Still a Secret (Esther 2:19–20)

Early in the story Esther demonstrates that she is compliant. Even though she is now the queen, she obeys Mordecai (Esth 2:20; see also 2:10). It was Esther's obedience that got her selected as queen in the first place. She is thus portrayed in stark contrast to the former queen, Vashti. But Esther's most significant contribution at this point in the storyline is her position in the palace.

Mordecai Exposes an Assassination Plot (Esther 2:21–23)

Mordecai then overhears an assassination plot against the king. Two of the king's officials are disgruntled for some undisclosed reason—yet another gap for the reader to fill (Esth 2:21). Mordecai demonstrates surprising loyalty to the throne by passing along news of this secret plot to Queen Esther, who in turn informs the king. Mordecai shows no hint of hostility against this foreign king, even though he himself is Jewish. His exposure of the plot showcases his trustworthy character and his respect for the authority of the throne.

After the account of the plot is checked out and confirmed, the offenders are taken to the gallows, revealing the ruthlessness with which the king handles opposition. However, Mordecai is for whatever reason (an oversight?) not recognized for his courageous foiling of the assassination plot. This creates yet another gap—one that will be filled in later in the story. Esther evidently makes no effort to ensure that Mordecai is rewarded, but this incident establishes a much-needed credibility for Esther in the king's sight, which will pay off later.

The King Honors the Jews' Enemy (Esther 3:1–5)

An undisclosed period of time passes before the king appoints Haman, thus far unmentioned in the story, to the place of highest honor in his kingdom. This is in stark contrast to Mordecai, who has as yet received no recognition for his services to the throne. The king, for undisclosed reasons, promotes Haman above everyone else (Esth 3:1). There is no indication that this is not a legitimate, deserved appointment. Haman's promotion to this lofty position creates the context for a crisis of epic proportions for the Jews, a crisis that is especially striking against the backdrop of Mordecai's commendable loyalty. Should he not have been promoted in place of Haman? This juxtaposition keeps the reader guessing as another gap is revealed. In the end there will be a switch that will seem to justify this line of thinking.

While no credentials are furnished concerning Haman's suitability for his new position, the response he commands is clear: "All the royal officials at the gate knelt down and paid honor to Haman, for the king had commanded this concerning him" (Esth 3:2). The king has honored him, so everyone else is expected to do the same.

Mordecai Refuses to Honor Haman (Esther 3:1–4)

However, again for undisclosed reasons, Mordecai refuses to honor Haman (Esth 3:2). Mordecai's rebuff cannot be traced back to any lack of respect for rightful rulers and their authority—he has just demonstrated loyalty to the king by saving his life. This is a significant gap in the story that generates suspense, and it will soon be filled in.

Just as Mordecai has informed the king about the assassination plot, these royal officials tattle on Mordecai to Haman (Esth 3:3–4). Predictably, Haman's response to Mordecai reflects the king's response to Vashti's defiance. At this point the storyteller again includes an "insignificant" detail about Mordecai's identity: He is Jewish (Esth 3:4).

A Legacy of Bad Blood Surfaces (Esther 3:5)

A little deeper investigation into the background of both of these key characters, Haman and Mordecai, reveals what may underlie Mordecai's blatant act of defiance, as well as Haman's personal but undisclosed vendetta against Mordecai and his people, the Jews.

The storyteller subtly informs us of Haman's identity (Esth 3:1) and in so doing offers us the key to understanding the bad blood that has existed between him and Mordecai: Haman is an Agagite!

The hostile opposition to Israel that has characterized the Amalekites of Israel's past still exists within the heart of Haman the Agagite, and he will stop at nothing short of annihilating the Jews if he has the chance—exactly the opportunity he now has in his new position of power.

It is important to note that Mordecai's defiance is not just a snub against Haman; he is defying the king's command. We recognize here a flashback to Queen Vashti's insubordination: Will Mordecai suffer the same dire consequences, or even worse? This gives

Haman grounds to execute his plan and demonstrate his power and superiority over Mordecai.

> **THE AMALEKITES VS. THE ISRAELITES**
>
> Generations earlier the Israelites had secured a memorable victory against the Amalekites—who had attacked them after their rescue from Egypt—when Moses lifted his hands to heaven to secure the victory over their enemies. Following this battle God had made his people a promise to wipe out the Amalekites (Exod 17:14). God reminded Israel later on, in Deuteronomy 25:17–19, that these Amalekites would be blotted out from under heaven. The inevitable confrontation had occurred under the leadership of King Saul, an ancestor of Mordecai (these details are recorded in 1 Sam 15:1–3). God commanded Saul to totally destroy the Amalekites, but Saul for whatever reason spared Agag, the Amalekite king (1 Sam 15:20; Samuel later killed Agag; see 1 Sam 15:33). Ironically, an Amalekite would later kill King Saul (2 Sam 1:1–16).

Haman Plots a Jewish Genocide (Esther 3:6–15)

Haman's anger spills over to extend not just to Mordecai but to all of Mordecai's people, the Jews (Esth 3:6). Haman's hostility is so passionate that he wants to wipe out the Jews everywhere in the vast Persian kingdom. This is, of course, in stark contrast to what God wants. So the duel is on: Who will get his way? The stakes are high: Within the bigger picture God's plan for salvation through a Jewish descendant is now also in jeopardy. How can he fulfill his plan if all Jews everywhere are to be annihilated?

> God's plan for salvation through a Jewish descendant is now in jeopardy. How can he fulfill his plan if all Jews everywhere are to be annihilated?

The Date with Fate Set (Esther 3:7)

The storyteller provides both the chronological year—the 12th of the king's reign—and the time frame for the Jewish genocide. The setting of the date is significant, as this appears to be a settled matter even prior to Haman's seeking the king's approval. Does this reflect a real power shift, indicating that Haman is calling the shots now? If so, this is detrimental to Mordecai and his fellow Jews.

Even more interesting, the date is not set by Haman personally but by lot—the *pur* (clay cubes like dice used for divination). This is how, later on in the story, the Jewish feast Purim will get its name. In other words, the date is set by the Persian gods.

A CLASH OF DEITIES

In Persian mythology, one of the gods, Ahuramazda (meaning "lord of wisdom"), was acknowledged as the creator and the god of light, truth, and goodness. This Persian god was also accredited with giving the Persian king his supreme rule over his vast empire.[2] However, the Jewish God Yahweh is the creator God, not merely of the Jews but of all people everywhere, and he rules over all creation. The clash of the deities was therefore inevitable.

So which deity will be the victor? Will the Persian gods decide the fate of God's people? Eleven months must pass before Haman's plan can come to fruition.

The King Decrees the Death Sentence (Esther 3:8–12)

Haman delivers a masterful sales pitch to the king (Esth 3:8–9), though he has to stretch the truth to provide what may sound like a valid reason to indict these "defiant" people. He paints an inaccurate picture of this unnamed people's disloyalty to the throne; an alleged disloyalty has already been disproven by Mordecai's revelation of the assassination plot. Note that none of Haman's trumped-up accusations against the Jews are evident in the lives of Esther and Mordecai; at this point in the story Esther's Jewish identity is still a secret. Interesting also is that Haman opts not to reveal the identity of these people to the king. What is most surprising is that the king makes no effort to identify them either. Haman sweetens the deal by offering a substantial cash injection into the royal coffers, betraying his absolute determination to eliminate the Jews at any price, as well as showing off his own substantial wealth (Esth 3:9). In this regard he apes the king.

The king acquiesces to Haman's request and gives him his signet ring, conferring upon Haman all the authority he could ever dream of to realize his genocidal plot. Berlin is of the opinion that the king's actions reveal that he is weak and easily manipulated.[3] In this action he essentially abdicates his role to rule.

At this critical point the storyteller exposes Haman's true identity: He is the antagonist in the story, the enemy of the Jews (Esth 3:10). In the name of the king, Haman issues a death decree applying to all Jews everywhere. Their fate is sealed! It appears that he is the victor in this conflict with Mordecai.

The Date with Fate Is Published Far and Wide (Esther 3:13–15)

The death decree is circulated to everyone in the whole kingdom, written in various dialects to ensure that everyone understands it.[4] This detail calls to mind the Tower of Babel, where human language was scrambled (Gen 11:7), as well as Pentecost's reversal thereof (Acts 2:8). The way the storyteller records the edict (Esth 3:13) reveals that it is intended to supersede the decree God had issued many years earlier (1 Sam 15:3). Another important element is that this is legally binding—especially since the law of the Medes and Persians cannot be repealed (Esth 1:19). This combination of factors poses a serious crisis. The very existence of the Jews is at stake, and there appears to be no escape. Haman has masterminded this genocide, and now it is just a matter of time before his edict is fulfilled. "Coincidentally," however, the death warrant is to be carried out on the 13th day. The very next day, however, will be Passover, which the Jews have long celebrated to commemorate God's deliverance of their ancestors in the past. This apparent fluke offers a glint of hope: God has delivered his people before; perhaps he will do so again.

The scene closes on a mixed note. The two most powerful men in the world are sitting together, smugly sipping wine, while the citizens of the capital city are, not surprisingly, alarmed by the breaking news. All of the Jews in the kingdom will be devastated. Many others in the empire will sympathetically mourn this impending, inevitable loss of life (yet another clue that the Jews are not universally despised). The very existence of the Jews is in jeopardy. How can they avoid being wiped off the face of the earth?

Fulfilling His Purposes

God's people should not be surprised when hostility is unexpectedly vented against them. Rather, we as Christians ought to be mindful that the real opponent of our faith lurks behind all human opposition, seeking to destroy us and our faith. But we can take courage in the fact that we serve a God who is able to ward off these attacks. Although life's circumstances may appear bleak, there is never a valid reason to surrender hope; our God is able to accomplish the impossible.

> Although life's circumstances may appear bleak, there is no valid reason to surrender hope, for God is able to do the impossible.

This scene also reminds us of the cost of other people's disobedience, which can "haunt" successive generations. My own disobedience and that of my generation can have a trickle-down effect in the lives of those who will follow. This realization ought to inspire us to greater obedience, motivating us to ensure that the legacy we leave behind for coming generations will not adversely compromise or cost them due to our failure to obey God.

We are also reminded that nothing "coincidental" ever happens in life. Even if the lot has been cast, seemingly reflecting the will of the "gods," nothing should deter us from trusting the true God to vindicate his people and so fulfill his ancient promises. Even though our situation may seem impossible, he *will* fulfill his purposes; nothing can thwart his plans. He will demonstrate his vast superiority over all other powers and over any plots.

SUGGESTED READING

- ☐ Esther 2:19–3:15
- ☐ Exodus 17:8–15
- ☐ Deuteronomy 25:17–19
- ☐ 1 Samuel 15
- ☐ 2 Samuel 1:1–16
- ☐ Proverbs 16:33

Reflection

How should you, as a Christian, react to the unexpected threats you face from time to time? How will knowing who is really behind these threats help you to more effectively withstand them (Eph 6:12)?

____

____

____

____

What trickle-down consequences might you, intentionally or unintentionally, have created for your descendants—your children and grandchildren—because of your disobedience to God?

____

____

____

____

How should you deal with seeming coincidences that happen in your life as a Christian (Prov 16:33)?

____

____

____

____

6

SCENE THREE: A JEWISH QUEEN TO THE RESCUE

God's people are now living under the threat of death, facing what appears to be an unavoidable genocide. Haman, the enemy of the Jews, holds the power as he waits for time to tick by until his plot can be fulfilled. But as the plot unfolds, it is evident once again that God places his people in just the right places at exactly the right times.

The King's Command Engenders Distress Everywhere (Esther 4:1–8a)

A crisis has flared up overnight in the capital city of Susa. Can you imagine the pandemonium as news circulates of the death sentence the king has decreed against all Jewish people? This is not simply a sentence for one particular person; it impacts the entire Jewish nation scattered far and wide throughout the Persian Empire. What words can begin to describe the impending horror? Understandably, the Jews respond to this news by mourning (Esth 4:1–3). Their response is reminiscent of the Ninevites' reaction to Jonah's message of doom: They cast themselves on God's compassion in repentance to spare them from destruction (Jonah 3:5–9).

The storyteller focuses on Mordecai's response, but others throughout the kingdom have similar reactions to this devastating news. You can imagine the talk on the streets, as everybody would have known about this impending threat. The Jews' dress code instantly alters. Everyone who is Jewish is walking around in sackcloth. Mordecai is even denied access beyond the king's gate because he is inappropriately dressed as a mourner. This is the first appearance of any feature that distinguishes the Jews from everyone else. The Jews' physical distinctiveness here can be compared to a cultural custom among Zulus living in South Africa, who cut marks on the faces of very young children with a razor, the resulting scars of which will identify their family heritage and distinguish them as belonging to a specific clan.

PROPER MOURNING

Wearing sackcloth as a garment was an outward expression of grief about a imminent disaster—a future threat—or as a show of mourning over someone's death or sorrow for sin (see Jonah 3:5). It was an uncomfortable garment to wear, yet affordable by all, and gave outward expression to inward emotions; this differs from today where emotions are expressed outwardly rather than by a specific dress code. As Berlin notes, "Fasting and sackcloth are probably not to be seen as specifically Jewish religious practices, but as universal expressions of mourning in the ancient Near East."[1]

Surprisingly, it does not appear that Queen Esther knows what is happening. She is clueless about this devastating turn of events—or so it appears. Upon learning that Mordecai is walking around dressed in sackcloth, she quickly sends him clothes (Esth 4:4).

Her ignorance is dispelled by an update from Mordecai, at her request (Esth 4:5). Mordecai provides her with every detail of this devastating development (Esth 4:6–8).

This news undoubtedly shakes Queen Esther, in spite of the fact that no one else knows she is Jewish. Although she is living in ostentatious luxury in the Persian king's palace, she must be distraught to learn that all Jewish lives are at risk—her own included. Mordecai will soon remind her of this, just in case she feels complacent and protected inside the palace. She will soon experience a clash of worlds: the Persian world against her Jewish heritage.

Mordecai Instructs Esther to Plead for Mercy from the King (Esther 4:8b–11)

Mordecai, recognizing the approaching disaster, puts Esther on the spot. This crisis will produce a transformation of her character as she puts her life on the line to save her people.[2] Esther grows in stature as the story progresses, and she becomes the dominant character, in spite of being a woman (Esth 1:20)—even to the point of directing her husband, the king, about what to do! Mordecai urges her to beg for mercy from the king (Esth 4:8b). After all, she lives in the king's palace and, on occasion, shares his bed. If anyone has access to the king's ear, it is she. Mordecai knows that this is a life-and-death issue, so Esther must plead for her life, as well as for the lives of her people, before the king. She has to use her royal position and her privilege as queen to gain access to the king's presence to save the lives of her fellow Jews. This is what Mordecai expects of Queen Esther. Will she come through?

Mordecai's request raises a fresh crisis. Even as queen, Esther does not have unrestricted access to the king's royal presence. The most likely reason for this restriction is to protect the king from any would-be assassins.[3] In this story he has already faced one assassination plot, which Mordecai exposed and foiled. My own country, South Africa, was rocked by the assassination of a political leader who was gunned down in a suburb neighboring our home. The assassination inculcated fear and threatened to plunge the country into a bloodbath, which mercifully was averted. Sadly, this occurrence has been repeated far too often worldwide throughout history.

The conversation between Esther and Mordecai is conducted by intermediaries. He appeals for her intervention, and in reply she outlines her new dilemma. In spite of her status as queen, she can see the king only when he calls for her; she cannot initiate an audience with him (Esth 4:11). To make matters worse, a full month has elapsed since she was last with the king. There is uncertainty about how much time will pass before he again requests her company. She cannot afford to wait—time is of the essence, as all Jewish lives are at stake.

Esther Risks Her Life to Enter the King's Presence Uninvited (Esther 4:12–16)

The king alone has the ability to save Queen Esther's life, but if she enters his presence uninvited she may meet with death anyway. Either way she faces a death sentence, though she has not yet disclosed her Jewish identity. Death seems inescapable—even for her in the palace. She is faced with a choice: Which way does she prefer to die? She may as well sacrifice her life for the cause of her people rather than try to keep silent about her identity. She is willing to transgress the law, and this leads to her famous statement: "if I perish, I perish" (Esth 4:16).

This is the first time in the story that Esther takes charge. Up to this point she has followed Mordecai's commands explicitly. Now she is exerting her authority, revealing a development in her character. She instructs Mordecai to institute a fast—implying that divine intervention is required—before she approaches the king. She further commands Mordecai to gather the doomed Jews together for a three-day vigil (Esth 4:15–17). This incident marks the beginning of a power shift: For the first time Mordecai carries out Esther's instructions. It has been the other way around for Esther's entire life.

You can imagine how fervently these Jews in Susa pray and fast, for their lives are on the line. Their request for deliverance is urgent. If ever God's help is required, it is now. So they deny themselves food—a fast (not a feast!)—to implore God to grant Queen Esther success in boldly approaching the king on their behalf. Esther promises to fast as well. This is possibly the first occasion in which her Jewish identity is exposed to her maids, who join her in the fast (Esth 4:16).

Mordecai Expresses Faith in God to Fulfill His Promises (Esther 4:14)

Listen carefully to Mordecai's words here (Esth 4:14). He is not a desperate-beyond-measure man. Yes, he knows his life is on the line, but for the first time he also reveals a deep trust in God. Absolutely nothing in this regard has been expressed thus far in the Esther story—with the recent exception of Esther's plea to get the people praying. This is the first clear evidence that Mordecai has an unwavering, unshakable trust in God—not in Esther or in her plea to the king (important though that may be). Even if Esther fails to take the initiative in this time of crisis and orchestrate a means of escape, this will not signal the end of all hope—that is never the case with God. God will never fail to deliver on his promises. He will never abandon his people. He will deliver them not because they are so good or so faithful to him (there has been no evidence of that thus far in the story), but for his own name's sake. Mordecai confidently asserts that, if needed, they will find another way of escape.

God will never fail to deliver on his promises. He will never abandon his people. He will deliver them not because they are so good or so faithful to him but for his own name's sake.

Will Esther succeed in her appeal to the king? Will Xerxes spare her life and accept her request favorably? Is Esther in the right place at the right time for God to use her to fulfill his purpose to deliver his people from death and destruction?

Esther Is Saved from Death (Esther 5:1–8)

Esther takes her life in her hands and hangs around in the king's courtyard. In contrast to all the other Jews, she is dressed in her royal robes.[4] Not surprisingly, the king catches a glimpse of his beautiful queen, and against all odds he grants her permission to come into his presence (Esth 5:1). He extends the gold scepter to her to indicate that she may approach him without fear of death (Esth 5:2). But this is merely the first step. Queen Esther's life is safe for the moment. She has negotiated the first hurdle well, but she—like all her fellow Jews—is still under a death threat. No one else in the palace knows this yet, however, for her identity has not yet been disclosed.

The King Grants Esther's Request (Esther 5:3)

How will Esther fare in the king's presence? Surely her heart must be pounding in her chest, but she has a plan. Having gained access to the king's presence, she finds favor with him (Esth 5:2 ESV)—again! Surely she has everything going for her now. Inexplicably, the king even asks her what she wants, and he assures her that he will offer her up to half his kingdom (Esth 5:3)—yet another extravagance.

Once she has the king's ear, Esther calms herself and invites him and Haman to a feast (Esth 5:4)—her own feast. She keeps the king in suspense regarding her request. This arrangement suits the arrogant Haman, who sees royal privilege extended to him yet again. This will providentially work in Esther's favor.

Esther Hosts a Feast (Esther 5:4–8)

We cannot be certain to what extent Esther had set up her survival plan in advance. Maybe her having a plan shows that she expected to be favorably received by the king—perhaps due to God's intervention in response to the fast. She creates a context to bring together the two most powerful men in the kingdom around one table in her presence (Esth 5:5), at which point she will make her next strategic move. She hosts the banquet where these two powerful men will sit and drink wine together (Esth 5:6); neither seems to have a concern in the world. Then she plays for time to draw out the suspense even more, making room for God to maneuver—yet again—by inviting the king and Haman to a second feast (Esth 5:8) at which she promises to make her request known to the king.

Esther is strategically placed in the palace to secure the deliverance of God's people. But she still has to ask the king to save the lives of the condemned Jewish people throughout the kingdom.

Confidence in God

Mordecai displays an astounding confidence that God will intervene to prevent the crisis. Likewise, we must show confidence in Christ, who will overrule circumstances and events for our ultimate benefit. We never know what God will do, yet we can be assured that he will intervene to ensure that his purposes are fulfilled.

We can express this confidence in prayer—asking for God's intervention and then believing it will be forthcoming. Prayer expresses a deep reliance upon God, especially when circumstances are far beyond our ability to cope with or effect change.

No power on earth or in heaven is able to thwart God's purposes. God will use whomever he wishes, wherever they are, to serve his purposes. He will strategically place them just where he needs them to be. Nothing happens by chance or coincidence.

> No power on earth or in heaven is able to thwart God's purposes.

Esther serves as an example of someone who is willing to sacrifice all to rescue her people—in spite of her royal position. This sacrificial character is epitomized in Jesus, who also forsook privilege—that of heaven—to come down to earth to rescue humanity from destruction. God's plan to rescue the world from the sentence of death and destruction was to send Jesus to deliver us through his own death (Rom 6:23).

The Esther story is a reminder that there are risks in openly declaring our core identity as Christians. But as God's people we should not fear to disclose our loyalty to Jesus—even if it costs us our life. Our confidence rests in God's promise to protect his people (John 10:28).

SUGGESTED READING

- ☐ Esther 4:1–5:8

Reflection

What gives you absolute confidence that God will intervene in your life for your good and for his glory?

___

___

___

___

What threats of death and destruction do you face in your daily life? How will you escape them?

___

___

___

___

What can you do to show that you are serious about seeking God's help in times of crisis?

___

___

___

___

7

SCENE FOUR: A JEW HONORED BY HIS ARCHENEMY

Evil will not triumph; God will not allow it to. God will, and already has, definitively overcome evil. The turn of events in this scene acts as proof. Here, the bitter feud between Mordecai the Jew and the newly appointed prime minister, Haman the Agagite, culminates in Haman abusing his power by issuing an irreversible death sentence for all Jews based on his intense hatred for Mordecai. But just when everything seems to be going according to Haman's script, the king's sleepless night changes everything and sets Haman hurtling on a course toward disaster and destruction. And totally unexpectedly the tide turns.

Haman's Advisers Propose the Execution of His Archenemy (Esther 5:9–14)

On his return from his exclusive feast with the king and queen, Haman runs into a defiant Mordecai yet again. Once more this provokes his anger (Esth 5:9). But he knows it is only a matter of time before his murderous plan is executed: All of the Jews, including

Mordecai, will soon be annihilated. So he heads home, restraining himself from lashing out against Mordecai's persistent noncompliance. The storyteller describes Haman's mood at the beginning of this episode (Esth 5:9) as joyful and happy. This is in stark contrast to his mood at the end of the episode (Esth 6:12).

> **WOMEN CHARACTERS**
>
> Women are often viewed as inferior and subservient to men in cultures ancient and modern. Yet God sovereignly chooses to use women to fulfill significant roles in accomplishing his purposes. And God has assigned the same status to men and women in his sight as both are made in his image (see Gen 1:27)—even though, by divine design, they fulfill a distinctive role within marriage (see Eph 5:22). The three women in the Esther story are excellent examples of how God uses women in his grand story and will continue to do so for his glory.

Haman Boasts before His Advisers (Esther 5:10–14)

Haman's conversation with his wife and friends is revealing. His boasts about his wealth and power recall the king's ostentatious displays in chapter 1. The storyteller attempts to afford us a glimmer of insight into Haman's hidden ambition through this glaring similarity—even though the two men's boasts are on a vastly different scale. Haman basks in the glory of his exclusive royal invitation from the queen (Esth 5:12), unaware that this will be his undoing.

It is ironic that Haman's wife, Zeresh, is now his adviser. It is unclear whether the storyteller intends for us to juxtapose this incident of a woman dominating her husband against the backdrop of the king's command and the ensuing events in chapter 1.

But for what other reason would the writer now mention Zeresh by name?[1] Haman's wife, together with his friends, encourages him to execute Mordecai—the sooner the better! These supporters are definitely on his side; like him, they are vehemently opposed to Mordecai. They hatch the plan to construct a gallows to make a public spectacle of Mordecai, who persistently dares to defy the king's command (see Esth 3:12). This would confirm Haman's supremacy and finally result in the elimination of his hated foe.

All the power in the Persian Empire has been vested in Haman by the king, yet he still requires the king's permission to authorize his plan. He does not expect resistance in securing the king's permission—particularly given that the edict to kill the Jews is already in effect (see Esth 3:13). There is only one bright spot missing in his life now: the satisfaction of bringing about Mordecai's death (see Esth 3:13). This outcome will be even more satisfying than his considerable wealth. Accordingly, with a smirk on his face, he issues the order to construct the gallows (the proportions of the gallows here are likely exaggerated to indicate that they will be visible for all to see).

Haman Seeks the King's Permission to Execute His Archenemy (Esther 5:14)

Off to the palace Haman goes to seek audience with the king to authorize his plan. He arrives at the palace, but before he gets an opportunity to ask the king to legalize his death sentence for Mordecai he is summoned into his presence to offer his sought-after advice. (Again, how ironic: His wife has just advised him what to do; now he has to advise the king!) But this unexpected summons denies him a chance to make his request of the king.

Haman's Unexpected Reversal of Honor (Esther 6:1–12a)

The storyteller dramatically recounts how Haman's plan to execute Mordecai is frustrated. The narrative becomes a tale of the reversal of fortunes—at Haman's expense—all triggered by events that have transpired in the king's life overnight, unknown to Haman.

The King's Bout of Insomnia (Esther 6:1–3)

The previous night the king had been unable to sleep (Esth 6:1). Whether he was mulling over what Esther's request might possibly be or whether other royal matters weighed heavily on his mind doesn't really matter. The storyteller chooses not to disclose the reason for the king's insomnia, once again creating a gap for the reader to ponder.

What he does during his bout of wakefulness is most surprising. Instead of just lying there, trying unsuccessfully to fall asleep, the king commands that the history books recording his reign be read aloud to him (Esth 6:1). This might seem to have been a rather vain and random remedy for sleeplessness, but the activity would probably have puffed him up and boosted his ego. From these records, he would have also been able to create a list of people who should receive honor.[2] To his shame Xerxes discovers that the man who has saved his life from an assassination plot some time ago has never been rewarded for this noble deed (Esth 6:2). Kuhrt informs us that "the king's favour was expressed through the bestowal of gifts: all privileges enjoyed emanated from the throne."[3]

What do you suppose were the chances that the king wouldn't have been able to find sleep on this precise evening? What were the chances that he would have decided to review the history of his reign? That he would hear about the incident of Mordecai saving his life? Surely this cannot have been coincidental. It is as though God were turning the pages. Is he not, after all, the lord of history?

Haman's Presumption about Honor Conferred (Esther 6:4–9)

The events that transpire at this point are tragi-comical. Haman is so full of himself that he presumes there is no one in the entire empire the king would rather honor except than himself; he is blissfully unaware of any possibility that the king might seek to dignify someone else. He answers all the questions presumptuously, with himself in mind. This results in the most absurd turnabout of fortunes.

Haman is desperate to receive acclaim that will further fuel his ambition and hunger for power. So he lays it on thick regarding the reward the king should bestow on the one he wishes to honor (Esth 6:6).

Unwittingly, by giving his advice to the king, Haman exposes his own insatiable desire for power and status. According to Haman the king should dignify the individual in question by allowing him to wear the king's own robe and ride his personal steed; for good measure he recommends that the king's most noble prince should parade the individual being honored through the streets. In essence, Haman is betraying his aspiration to *be* the king. The ugly side of his rugged ambition is exposed. The only thing belonging to the king he does not propose to have is his queen. Ironically, this issue will soon play itself out as well. But little does Haman recognize that this proposal will have a boomerang effect.

To Haman's horror the king assigns honor to Haman's archenemy, Mordecai—the very man Haman has been plotting to execute. What a bizarre turn of events. Haman has come to the palace to ask the king's permission to execute Mordecai; now he ends up giving him advice that results in Mordecai receiving the honor Haman felt that he himself deserved.

Mordecai Is Honored; Haman Is Humiliated (Esther 6:10–12a)

The king commands Haman to publicly parade his nemesis, Mordecai, through the streets of Susa, shouting, "This is what is done for the man the king delights to honor" (Esth 6:11). This must have been the most mortifying event of Haman's life. After having been appointed prime minister and so vested with power and prestige, he finds himself having to be the one to publicly shout Mordecai's praise. Worse still, the public is enthralled with Mordecai, the hero. Ironically, Haman is publicly promoting Mordecai's cause against the bleak backdrop of the highly public gallows he has constructed for this same man's demise.

The king, for his part, delights in honoring someone who has saved his life; he knows that Mordecai is a Jew (Esth 6:10) but is blissfully unaware that his life is under threat by an edict he himself has issued.

Mordecai recognizes that his life is still on the line, and even though he is being paraded triumphantly through the streets he would gladly exchange this honor for his life—and those of his people. Then Mordecai returns to his post at the king's gate (Esth 6:12).

It seems highly likely that some, and maybe many, citizens of Susa would by now have heard about Haman's murderous plot against Mordecai, especially with the highly visible gallows having been constructed in full view of all. Haman would have been utterly humiliated by this highly visible procession in honor of Mordecai. The storyteller subtly indicates that the tide has turned against Haman. Who is orchestrating this unpredictable turnaround?

The storyteller is subtly indicating that the tide has turned against Haman. Who is orchestrating this unpredictable turnaround?

Haman hurries home, where he expects to find support, only to find out otherwise.

Haman's Advisers Predict His Downfall (Esther 6:12b–14)

While Haman is blind to his impending ruin, his advisers are all too aware that he will not succeed. The storyteller does not disclose what has caused Haman's wife and friends to change their minds so radically overnight. This gap yet again leaves readers to ponder. Haman's family is aware of Mordecai's Jewish heritage, but they now seem to realize that Haman cannot outmaneuver Mordecai—or is it Mordecai's God? Is this their declaration of surrender, realizing that Mordecai's God is superior to their Persian gods? As Jobes writes:

> Read in a polytheistic context, the story suggests that Yahweh, the God of the Jews, had overpowered Haman's gods in this instance. Read from a monotheistic perspective, the story explains the reversal of fortune not as an ongoing tug-of-war between the gods, but as consistent with the powerful word of the one, true God.[4]

Is there any possibility that Haman's erstwhile supporters are aware of the fate God had much earlier prescribed for Haman's ancestors—that they recognize themselves to be under judgment from Mordecai's God? Is this unexpected turn of events really the end of the road for Haman? Either way, his advisers now recognize that he is fighting a losing battle. They could have seen his defeat coming from miles away, and they predict that he will come to ruin. He has shifted from being in total control, with the king's signet ring in his possession, to being forced to lead this humiliating public charade. The cracks are beginning to show; he seems to be facing a dismal end. With Mordecai being honored, how can Haman now request permission from the king to execute him? How inexplicably matters have turned around.

As readers we can see what is happening: No opponent can take on God and expect to win. God is providentially at work in everyday life to fulfill his promises. Evil will not triumph; God will vindicate his people, and evil will be destroyed.

No adversary can take on God and expect to win. God will vindicate his people, and evil will be destroyed.

Ultimate Victory

Ever since the initial entrance of rebellion into God's perfect world God has promised that he will rescue his people from sin and reverse its deadly effects. And he has, supremely, done this through Jesus' death on the cross, upon which the Son surrendered his life to rescue those trapped in sin and under the sentence of death.

God does not abandon his people, and he ultimately reigns over all of history. But this does not mean that wicked people won't perpetrate evil that will deeply affect our lives; likewise, it doesn't mean that God's people will be spared from catastrophe. But the symptoms of our broken world do not indicate that God is powerless to act. God can use even those seemingly little things in life to effect a turnaround of fortunes; in the Esther story the sleeplessness of the king is God's doing, an essential part of his plan to save his people.

I recall a recent incident in which my wife arranged to meet her niece at a shopping mall. She had intended to go shopping afterward but instead returned home to fetch something for her niece. Upon her arrival she found plumes of smoke billowing from the house. In her haste to leave she had inadvertently forgotten to turn off a stovetop burner. Had her plans not changed our home would have gone up in flames! Such averting of a disaster can be, and in this case I'm firmly convinced was, evidence of God's unseen hand at work.

Haman is the very picture of evil—he is evil personified. We see him as a picture or type of the evil one who opposes God's people, willing to do anything to destroy them. We ought to be aware of the evil one's sinister, deadly strategy. His aim is to destroy our faith in Christ so that we will abandon our faith (John 10:10). The reversal of fortunes in Esther prefigures God's ultimate reversal of evil, when his people will at last be vindicated and his enemies forever destroyed (Rev 20:7–10).

> The reversal of fortunes in Esther prefigures God's ultimate reversal of evil, when his people will be vindicated and his enemies destroyed (Rev 20:7–10).

Even God's enemies recognize their inevitable defeat. They cannot outwit or outmaneuver God—try though they may. God had decreed that those ancient enemies, the Amalekites, who had dared so long ago to oppose his people, would be annihilated. Haman, the Agagite, thought he had a chance to turn the tables and eliminate all of God's people—only to discover that he was powerless to do so. God's enemies know that defeat is inevitable and that final judgment and terrible destruction await them. There is only one solution to escape this judgment: switch sides. Instead of opposing God and his people they should join God's people and escape the coming wrath (1 Thess 5:9).

SUGGESTED READING

- ☐ Esther 5:9–6:13
- ☐ 2 Thessalonians 1:5–10
- ☐ Revelation 12:7–12

Reflection

How has God reversed your life's fortunes? How is this change evident in your everyday life?

____

____

____

____

When have you seen God at work in your everyday life with regard to people you meet and circumstances you face? Can you think of times in your life when God has intervened with his impeccable timing?

How does the assurance of the defeat and doom of the evil one affect the way you live your life as a Christian day by day?

8

SCENE FIVE: A DEAD END FOR THE JEWS' ENEMY

Justice will prevail. For whatever reason, many people escape justice in this world. But this trend will not continue forever. God sees everything, and he will in his own time bring evil and its perpetrators to justice. This truth is a great comfort to those who endure unjust treatment. And in this scene, we see God's justice for Haman.

> God sees everything, and he will bring evil and its perpetrators to justice.

Queen Esther has hosted an exclusive feast for the king and Haman. The king has asked his beautiful queen what she wants, and she has delayed her answer twice already—in spite of his extremely generous offer. As she makes her request she reveals a well-kept secret that will both shock and instill fear in the king and Haman.

Esther Entreats the King to Save Her Life (Esther 7:3–8)

Esther has on numerous occasions won the king's favor; this has to be God's doing. But when she spills the beans about the dreadful threat to her life, she does not anticipate additional favor. She has to tread delicately so as not to imply that the king is complicit in this death edict. After all, he was the one who unwittingly permitted Haman to issue it.

Esther Reveals Her Jewish Identity (Esther 7:3–4)

Up to this point the king has been blissfully unaware that his queen's life is under threat. After all, he evidently hasn't so much as inquired about the identity of the people whose lives are at risk (see Esth 3:8). Even if he had asked Haman's clarification on this matter, he would still be unaware of his queen's nationality. Esther explains that, even now, she would have kept silent (see Esth 4:14) had this not been such a dire crisis (Esth 7:4b).

The king is shocked by Esther's revelation that her life is on the line. He demands to know who would have dared to threaten his own queen without his knowledge. His mind may even be flashing back to the assassination plot Mordecai had uncovered against him. Now there seems to be yet another plot—this time directed against his queen. But this plot does not merely affect Esther; it is against her people too. This is a serious situation; if carried out, the provisions of the decree will wipe the Jews throughout the Persian Empire off the face of the earth—and that fate will include the queen and Mordecai, who has just been publicly honored by the king. Esther uses the words of the death edict (see Esth 3:13) to explain her predicament to her husband (Esth 7:4a).

Xerxes is incensed that someone has dared to threaten the existence of Esther's people (Esth 7:5). He has twice promised Esther that he will grant her request, yet he faces a conundrum: He cannot both keep his promise to Esther and revoke the death edict he has unwittingly issued. Esther then masterfully exposes Haman as the villain. This is the climactic moment in the story.

Haman Begs Esther to Save His Life (Esther 7:7–8a)

The king, true to character, seethes with anger and leaves the banquet table to cool off. Michael V. Fox writes:

> We are not told why he does so, but we can grasp the quandary he faces. Can he punish Haman for a plot he himself approved? If he does so, won't he have to admit his own role in the fiasco? Moreover, he has issued an irrevocable law; how then can he rescind it?[1]

Haman, recognizing that his fate is sealed with the king, is left to the sole mercy of the queen. Perhaps he can save his life by appealing to Queen Esther. He must surely recognize that his appeals are unlikely to be heard, that Esther is setting him up before the king to spare her own life, along with those of her people. A switch of fortunes has occurred: At first it was Queen Esther trying to preserve her life; now Haman is scrambling to get out from under the wrath of the king.

How ironic that he who hates the Jews so intensely is now groveling before a Jewish woman—albeit a Persian queen—to spare his skin. The tide has turned, and definitively so. God has so orchestrated these events that this development will simultaneously lead to the saving of the Jews and the demise of the once-powerful Haman.

The tide has turned. God has so orchestrated these events that this development will simultaneously lead to the saving of the Jews and the demise of the once-powerful Haman.

Haman Is Gripped by the Fear of Death (Esther 7:8b)

Haman's downfall is swift. From his lofty position as prime minister, wielding power on the king's behalf to decree edicts, he falls from grace.

THE ROYAL COURT

The Persian royal court was made up of many people with the king as the central figure. The king lived in privacy in the palace with only his mother and wife. Only representatives of various prestigious nobles had access to his presence. Such restricted access to the king was to protect him from any assassination attempts. Within the king's court, the prime minister was the most powerful and influential individual. He had access to the king's presence and was allowed to rule the empire alongside the king. He enjoyed the confidence of the king and was his most valued adviser. Little else is known about the Persian courts.[2]

And then, as Xerxes returns from the garden, the king "conveniently" discovers Haman in what appears to be a compromising position—though it is likely not Haman's intention to harm Esther. The king now has grounds to execute Haman. If Haman's fate was not sealed before, it surely is now.

The King Does Not Save Haman's Life (Esther 7:9–10)

Haman's decline has been evident, and now the situation gets decidedly worse: His murderous plot boomerangs back on him as the king discovers that he has constructed a gallows on which to hang Mordecai.

The king's life has been saved by Mordecai, Esther's life has already been spared once by her capricious husband, and now Esther has asked the king to preserve both her life and those of her people. This is the wish the king has promised to grant her.

Xerxes promptly executes the wicked Haman; the villain gets his just deserts—ironically, on his own gallows. In the story's opening scene the king, in anger, has deposed his queen for her contempt of his authority; now, in rage, he demands Haman's life. Kuhrt notes that "rebellion, betrayal of trust, corrupt practices led to the public withdrawal of royal favour, signaled by the offender being stripped of his court ornaments ... in very serious cases, followed by public and horrific executions or slow death by torture."[3]

The evil one has been eliminated, but the threat to Jewish lives remains. How can these people be spared?

Just as the deposed queen made space for a replacement

queen, now there is a vacancy for a prime minister. Who will it be? Haman has been disgraced, exposed as a perpetrator of evil, and executed. The evil one has been eliminated, but the threat to Jewish lives remains. How can these people be spared?

Relying on God's Justice

The Esther story confirms that, in the end, wicked people will certainly experience shame and condemnation when they come face to face with God on the judgment day. There will be no place they can hide to escape God's intense and justified wrath. Even worse than death itself will be the second death—to be cast out of God's presence forever, banished irrevocably from his grace, mercy, and goodness. When Jesus returns, his enemy will at long last face his inevitable doom. Satan was publicly defeated at Christ's cross, but his ultimate end is still to come (Rev 20:10). His final destruction awaits him; just as surely as Haman was executed with everyone witnessing his demise, so the devil and his minions will be condemned eternally!

In this world there are many who, like Haman, are evil to the core, their wickedness evidenced by their hatred of anyone who belongs to God. They express their opposition to Christians to varying degrees—from mild distaste to murderous hatred, and every gradation in between. God's people are not always spared from malevolent people. We ought to expect the hatred of the world; just as his adversaries hated Jesus they will despise and persecute those who belong to him. Yet the presence of evil is no indication that God is powerless against its forces; in his flawless new creation no evil will be resident (Rev 21:27). In the meantime, we live in a fallen, broken world that is permeated by the presence and tragic effects of sin.

SUGGESTED READING

- ☐ Esther 7:1–10
- ☐ Mark 5:1–20
- ☐ 2 Thessalonians 1:5–10
- ☐ 2 Peter 2:4–9

Reflection

When you face evil in your life, how are you reassured by your knowledge of the future demise of the evil one and all who follow him?

____

____

____

____

Have you ever felt robbed or violated by the injustices of life? Where do you look to find hope for justice?

____

____

____

____

How does Esther's strategy to expose the evil threat against her life and the lives of her people encourage you to action in response to the plight of persecuted Christians worldwide?

___

___

___

___

9

SCENE SIX: A ROYAL EDICT SAVES THE JEWS

The king has unwittingly, through Haman, issued an irrevocable death decree. Even though Haman's life has ended, the king's edict remains in force. But God has providentially positioned two significant Jews in the palace to bring about a reversal of fortunes for his people and to spare them from destruction.

God has providentially positioned two significant Jews in the palace to bring about a reversal of fortunes for his people and to spare them from destruction.

Jews in the King's Palace (Esther 8:1–8)

On the same day the king sentences Haman to death for his iniquitous plot against the Jews he obliterates all traces of Haman's existence. (As though to ensure that the message has been clear, the storyteller one final time describes Haman as the Jews' enemy [Esth 8:1].) But even though Haman has been eliminated, the threat he had masterminded is still in effect—courtesy of a thorny provision in the law of the Medes and the Persians (Esth 8:3). Ironically, Mordecai is presented with the king's signet ring (Esth 8:2), indicating that he himself now holds in his hands all authority in the empire—authority that has been stripped away from the disgraced and deposed Haman. Mordecai too finds favor with the king. Later we learn once again that Mordecai is honored by the king (Esth 8:15)—ironically, Xerxes confers on him the very position Haman has held.

The estate of the disgraced Haman is confiscated, and the king awards all Haman's possessions to Esther. The queen, in turn, passes along Haman's considerable property to Mordecai (Esth 8:1–2). Still, however, in spite of the wealth he now possesses and the great honor bestowed on him by the king, Mordecai's life is on the line because he is a Jew. The underlying crisis still cries out for resolution.

For the first time in the story, Esther reveals the nature of her relationship with Mordecai (see Esth 7:4). Imagine how surprised the king must have been to discover this family link! But this revelation serves only to compound the crisis both Mordecai and Esther face (Esth 8:3, 6).

Esther once again pleads for the lives of the Jews. The king is "powerless" to save them (this is not the first time he finds himself entrapped by his own command); he must find some other way to avert or reverse the threat. The king extends his scepter to Esther for a second time in the story (Esth 8:4); again her life is spared, but can she in her turn spare the lives of the Jews?

Esther prefaces her appeal to the king with three conditions: If she has found favor with him, if it is the right thing to do, and if he is pleased with her. We can only conjecture that she must be confident these preconditions have been met. She is bold enough at this point even to suggest to the king a method for saving the Jews from destruction. Esther is portrayed as taking the initiative in the preservation of her own—of God's own—people (Esth 8:5). Speaking on behalf of herself and Mordecai, she asks the king to issue an overruling edict, which he does (Esth 8:8), indicating thereby that Mordecai and Esther have presumed on a favorable response to their request. Is this an act of faith in God? We can only assume that Esther has given much thought to how she can protect these Jewish lives.

Another Irrevocable Edict Is Issued (Esther 8:9–17)

It is evident that Mordecai's official title is now "the Jew"; both royals are here referred to by their royal titles (Esth 8:7). Rather than being despised for his Jewish background, Mordecai now wears his identity as a badge of honor. This honor will be confirmed when he is acclaimed by the king at the conclusion of the story (Esth 8:15). The tide has turned and the rescue plan hatched; now that plan needs only to be implemented.

Mordecai Issues the Counter-Edict (Esther 8:9–11)

With Haman no longer a hindrance, Mordecai—now vested with royal power to thwart the evil plot his nemesis had instituted—takes decisive action (Esth 8:10). The king has authorized the counter-edict (Esth 8:8), which is also irrevocable. Precisely as before, this edict is issued to the entire empire. A subtle change is that it now specifically addresses the Jews (Esth 8:9); this is hardly surprising, given the dire threat they face.

The date of this edict (Esth 8:9) reveals that the Jews' date with fate is scheduled nine months from that day, affording them ample time to prepare for the threat the first edict still poses to their existence. The counter-edict allows the Jews the right to gather—no doubt to plot their tactics for protecting themselves from hostile onslaught—and grants them the same powers the first edict conferred upon their enemies (Esth 8:11). If attacked, they are authorized to counter-attack to defend their lives. Berlin comments that "the second decree is not so much to give the Jews permission to defend themselves as to serve as a deterrent to those who might attack them."[1]

The Edict Comes into Effect on the 13th (Esther 8:12–17)

The counter-edict is slated to take effect on the same day as the first—the 13th (Esth 8:12). As proof that Mordecai, together with Esther, has successfully engineered the Jews' preservation, he departs the palace with royal honor (Esth 8:15).[2] The response in the capital city starkly contrasts with that evoked by the first edict: Sadness is transformed into gladness (Esth 8:15–17). Although the celebration may seem premature, the radically altered mood suggests that victory is a *fait accompli*. Jewish fortunes have been reversed, and fasting gives way to feasting (Prov 11:10).

The storyteller informs us that many (though not all) people of other nationalities are gripped by a fear of the Jews (Esth 8:17). Remarkably, this was precisely what had happened when God liberated the Israelites from Egypt. This fear implied that the superiority of God's people had been established—or was it that the superiority of their behind-the-scenes but ever-present and active God was being recognized at last? Was the people's fear of the Jews an indication that many had transferred their allegiance to the Jews' God? Might this have been a situation like that reflected in Ruth's words to Naomi: "Your people will be my people and your God my God" (Ruth 1:16)?

Berlin reminds us that a sign of conversion to Judaism—back then and still today—is circumcision. Since this rite is not mentioned here, it is unlikely that the situation in Persia involved a mass conversion.[3] The most probable explanation for this healthy fear seems to have been a prevailing knowledge that if the Jews were attacked they would fight back, probably ably, given the nature of the provocation. Further, the presence in the court of the honored Mordecai and Queen Esther, both Jewish, no doubt contributed to the reserve of those who might otherwise have dared to play the aggressors. Haman's demise had surely served as a further disincentive to wage war, though a defiant minority would still rise up to initiate a fight they had no hope of winning. But it would prove pointless to rise up against the Jews, who were now "licensed to kill." The king and his Persian military were in no way opposed to the Jewish residents of their land.

A Jewish Victory (Esther 9:1–17)

The storyteller reminds his readers that the doomsday envisaged for the destruction of the Jews has arrived but points out that it fails to materialize (Esth 9:1). Instead, the Jews gain the upper hand over those who despise them. Their enemies demonstrate their hatred in their obstinate preparation for a fight that can only result in their own destruction. The storyteller states it succinctly: "The tables were turned" (Esth 9:1). This is the greatest reversal in this story of reversals.

The Jews Prove Unbeatable (Esther 9:5)

A ludicrously lopsided battle erupts throughout the empire as the Jews mercilessly defeat their detractors. While this picture of destruction might seem to indicate that the Jews are gruesome and vindictive, it is more helpful to envision them merely protecting themselves from death—precisely as the edict has authorized them to do. They do not instigate the fight but respond effectively to hostile attack; once engaged in battle, they are invincible.

Their Enemies Are Wiped Out (Esther 9:6–17)

The battle statistics are alarming. In the capital city the Jews' enemies are roundly defeated—500 citizens are declared to be dead, with Haman's 10 sons listed among the casualties (Esth 9:7–10). They go the same route as the disgraced Haman, ending up not only humiliated but suspended, like their evil sire, high upon

Haman's gallows. Their bodies, just like his, are on display to remind everyone what will happen to those who dare to defy the king's (counter) edict—to anyone who might venture to attack the Jews. This confrontation effectively ends Haman's evil legacy; that the storyteller mentions all of his sons by name verifies that all of them are gone. This is a graphic picture of what happens to anyone who dares to take on God or his people.

The Jews do not take plunder, though they are legally entitled to it (this is surely evidence that they are not exacting revenge but merely defending themselves).

WARFARE SPOILS

Taking the plunder after a victory in battle was a common practice in ancient warfare (see Exod 3:22; Josh 8:27; 11:14); it was customary for the victors to take anything and everything as a reward. The battle plunder served as an incentive to conquer enemies—victors would gain their opponents' wealth as well as expand their own territory. It would be humiliating for the vanquished enemy to have to surrender everything after defeat. And taking the plunder would then effectively neutralize any efforts the defeated party might have to wage war against the victor.

This at last settles the ancient rivalry between Saul and the Amalekites (see 1 Sam 15). As Berlin points out:

> The Jews of Persia "correct" Saul's error. Saul took the booty from the Amalekites although he was forbidden to do so; but

> the Jews of Persia do not take booty from their enemies even though they are entitled to do so. If the feud between Haman and Mordecai is viewed as an extension of the dispute between Agag and Saul, this reversal in reference to booty wipes away the sin of the house of Saul. There is now nothing to prevent a complete triumph of the descendants of Saul over the house of Agag. And indeed, this is what happens in Mordecai's defeat of Haman and in the Jews' defeat of their Haman-inspired enemies.[4]

The king offers Esther yet another request (Esth 9:12), and she asks for another battle day—one that will result in even more casualties. Her request can only be viewed against the backdrop of God's threat against the Amalekites (see Exod 17:14). In this additional battle day the city of Susa is purged of the Jews' enemies. This decisive victory irrevocably proves that God keeps his word. The massive fatalities throughout the empire (Esth 9:16) need to be viewed in the same way. Having gained the victory, the Jews rest and celebrate their triumph.[5]

This decisive victory irrevocably proves that God keeps his word.

The Jews Celebrate Their Victory over Their Enemies (Esther 9:18–10:3)

A victory like this must never be short-lived; it must be celebrated in remembrance of all that God has done. That is why Mordecai issues instructions to observe an annual remembrance celebration (Esth 9:20–22). This is to be a time of feasting, not fasting, a time of joy and gladness, not sadness. This celebration will include the giving of gifts—a rich symbol of God's gift of deliverance of the Jews.[6] Fox notes that the giving of gifts "has a function beyond the charitable supplying of needs, namely the creation of a symbolic communal banquet to which everyone is invited."[7] Surely this prefigures the great banquet in heaven (see Rev 19:9).

The Feast Is to Remind Them of Their Rescue (Esther 9:23–26)

The Jews are never to forget God's deliverance; this is why the feast is instituted. They willingly consent to perpetuate the celebration to commemorate their deliverance. The storyteller then recounts the events in a condensed form that focuses on the threat Haman has posed to the Jews' existence (Esth 9:24–25).

Its Origin Is in the Name: "Purim" (Esther 9:24–28)

Purim means "lot." Haman resorted to pagan superstition and his pagan gods to determine when the destruction of the Jews was to occur; now "Purim" reminds them how the true and living God countered this threatened annihilation. It is not by chance that the Jews are saved; God saves them. This is precisely what the Jews are never to forget. All of the Jews are ready to commemorate God's rescue from annihilation—just as their ancestors celebrated the Passover to remember God's rescuing them from bondage in Egypt.

It Is a Royal Decree (Esther 9:29–10:3)

Queen Esther has the last word, confirming in a letter the authorization to celebrate Purim. Mordecai in his official capacity dispatches this letter to the entire empire. This serves to legalize the celebration of Purim for all the Jews.

This final chapter, in its brevity, serves as the epilogue, wrapping up the story beyond the Purim events.[8] The narrative that started with the king's lavish feasts concludes with his imposing taxes—his sovereign right. This action indicates his power, as well as the source of his prosperity. The royal records chronicle not Xerxes' prestige alone but also that of Mordecai (Esther is not mentioned). Mordecai receives credit for his care of the Jews—no doubt a reference to his initiating Esther's successful appeal to the king to spare their people from destruction. The Jews have been saved from eradication; surely this is God's doing, though he is not mentioned.

Mordecai the Jew is renowned throughout the Persian Empire for his work that resulted in the deliverance of God's people from death and destruction (Esth 10:3). Unlike Esther, who merely demonstrated her willingness to sacrifice her life for her people, Jesus Christ *did* sacrifice his life in death on the cross to pay the ultimate price for sin to deliver everyone who believes in him from death and destruction.

Rescued from Death

God will defeat every adversary. The demise of Haman, the enemy of the Jews, is swift: He is hanged alongside his own house. And all 10 of his sons come to the same dismal end he did. Those who hate the Jews experience considerable fatalities, but the storyteller mentions no loss of life among Jews in this battle across the vast empire. This is a convincing victory for God's people and a decisive defeat of all their enemies. It is a vivid yet stark reminder that every enemy of God's people, and of God himself, will certainly be defeated. There will be only one winner. God alone will triumph in the end.

The story of Esther further serves as a reminder that life's fortunes, in either direction, can be reversed. This is precisely what Jesus has done for us on the cross, where he gave his life as a ransom for sin so that our fortunes might be reversed from death and judgment to life. Christ died to rescue us from sin's consequences and to spare us from God's condemnation. Only God's king, Jesus, can rescind the edict of death and issue a counter-edict for life.

Jesus instituted the Lord's Supper (Holy Communion) to help us remember our rescue, which he accomplished for us on the cross (1 Cor 11:25).

The Jews have never been able to forget what God accomplished on their behalf in rescuing them from death and annihilation. However, there is another feast for Christians to remember: We celebrate a far greater rescue that God accomplished for all his people through Jesus' death on the cross. He commands us to commemorate this pivotal event of human history until he returns. Jesus instituted the Lord's Supper (Holy Communion) to help us remember the rescue he accomplished for us (1 Cor 11:25).

SUGGESTED READING

- ☐ Esther 8:1–10:3
- ☐ Romans 6:23
- ☐ 1 Corinthians 11:17–26
- ☐ 2 Thessalonians 1:5–10
- ☐ Revelation 21:1–5

Reflection

In what ways has God given you hope amid the despair and difficulties of life, transforming your sadness into gladness (Matt 5:11–12; Acts 13:48; 1 Pet 2:10; Rev 19:7)?

____

____

____

____

How does your life tell the story of the profound reversal of fortune wrought through Christ (Rom 5:6–8)?

____

____

____

____

What steps can you take as a Christian to meaningfully remember God's deliverance?

____

____

____

____

10

CONCLUSION

Many people today demand proof of God's existence. The Bible, however, simply assumes his presence (Gen 1:1). If God is not visible, if there is no obvious evidence he is there, if he is not talked about or even mentioned, he is often deemed not to exist. This attitude could be seen to be portrayed in the Esther story, in which God is not mentioned by name, or even alluded to, even once. But in the words of Barry Webb, "God is present even when he is most absent."[1] And the uniqueness of God's role in the Esther story is that he is at work in the ordinary aspects of everyday life. He uses the unexpected events of daily life and life's circumstances—sometimes even the inexplicable responses of people and their decisions—to achieve his purposes.

The God Who Is Invisible—Yet Profoundly Present

God's presence with his people is evident throughout Scripture. In Genesis God walks with Adam and Eve in the cool of the day (Gen 3:8). Later, in the exodus story, God's presence is evident from his works of deliverance and from the words—including some audible words—he speaks to his people, but most especially from the pillar of fire by night and of cloud by day. But after God's judgment against his people for their rebellion, resulting in exile from the promised land, God's people were concerned about what they construed as his lack of manifestation among them. Is God's presence restricted to the promised land? This unspoken question is part of the uniqueness of the Esther story, for some exiled Jews had not returned to their homeland and were living under foreign powers—in this case, in Persia. Could they be assured of God's availability and preservation outside the promised land? The Esther story gives these Jewish exiles a renewed confidence in God's working among them, even while they live in a foreign land under foreign powers. It also gives its readers, wherever they find themselves, faith that God is truly present with his people until the culmination of that glorious day when they will live in his eternal presence.

Even though God does not seem present in the book of Esther, the storyteller uses the narrative to show the ways in which he is at work in his creation.

God's Providence

The Esther story is littered with evidence of God's invisible presence—his fingerprints are everywhere. There are no coincidences in life; those very events we view as coincidental attest that God is at work in his world. Almost every scene has some remarkable twist or turn whereby God superintends

The Esther story is littered with evidence of God's invisible presence—his fingerprints are everywhere.

events and people for his own glory and for the good of his people. The wise teacher of Proverbs reminds us that "the lot is cast into the lap, but every decision is from the Lord" (Prov 16:33). This providential ruling of God is evident even in the destruction edict determined by the *pur*, which God graciously neutralizes to preserve his people's existence. God also determines how the powerful rulers of the nations of the world will govern: "The king's heart is in the hand of the Lord; he directs it like a watercourse wherever he pleases" (Prov 21:1). This gives incredible hope to all believers that God directs his world sovereignly, even though his presence may not be detected. Bruce Milne helpfully explains:

> God's providence means the ultimate triumph of his purposes is assured. All forces of opposition to God, sin and evil, corruption and injustice, greed and exploitation and the rest are held by God, kept in check by his providential reign, and are in the last analysis of merely temporary significance, no matter how impressive they may appear at present.[2]

This truth transforms the Christian's life because we are not to despair or abandon hope, for God is providentially at work in his world and in our lives; his plans will all come to fruition in his perfect timing (Gal 4:4).

God is providentially at work in his world and in our lives; his plans will all come to fruition in his perfect timing (Gal 4:4).

God's Victory

God is the ultimate victor. This is graphically portrayed in the last book of the Bible, Revelation. In spite of his enemies' hostile opposition to God and his people, God is the victor. He wins in the end (Rev 17:14). God's people savor this same note of triumph in the Esther story. The book of Esther describes an evil plot to eliminate the Jews, but God, the victor, will not allow this to happen. He overrules the evil threat against his people and secures their lasting preservation. God neutralizes the threat of genocide against the Jews; he not only gives them the upper hand against their enemies but also destroys the threat represented by Haman and all the forces allied with him against the Jews.

God is guaranteed victory over sin; this was secured by Christ's death on the cross, where he triumphed over his enemy (Col 2:15). This victory is also assured for all those who are on his side.

This truth transforms the Christian's life as it affords us the assurance that if we are on God's side we are on the winning side. Not a single enemy will triumph against him. He has defeated the devil on the cross—sin has been paid for—and he has defeated death by his resurrection. Our confidence must rest solely in him, for he has defeated our foes.

Our confidence must rest solely in him, for he has defeated our foes.

God's Promises

God made a promise to Adam that from Eve's womb a descendant would come who would defeat Satan, that evil one who had deceived Adam and Eve, and in so doing had led all of humanity astray. Jesus was that ultimate descendant who fulfilled this promise. Prior to his birth the angel from heaven announced to Mary: "You will give birth to a son, and you are to give him the name Jesus, because he will save his people from their sins" (Matt 1:21).

Later God promised Abraham, the father of the Jewish nation, that he would bless him and give him many descendants, as well as the land of promise (Gen 12:2–3). In the Esther story some of the descendants of Abraham, the Jews, are no longer living in the promised land; they are scattered in exile as a result of God's righteous judgment. But even though they are no longer in their homeland, they are still God's people, through whom he will continue to work out his purposes. The threat of their annihilation imperiled the promises he had made to Abraham, for God had promised that through Abraham's seed a descendant would come who would liberate the world from bondage to sin and destruction. God's promise of a rescuer from sin would be in jeopardy if all the Jews were annihilated.

Even later God promised King David that he would have a descendant on the throne forever (2 Sam 7:16). There was a time when this promise seemed to be on shaky ground—when Israel failed to have a king on the throne because God's people were in exile. But God, ever true to his word, kept his promise, and King Jesus was born of David's line (Luke 1:32–33).

This truth transforms the Christian's life because God has kept all of his promises to date, imbuing us with confidence that he will keep all of the promises he has made that are yet to be fulfilled. For one, he has pledged to forgive the sins of those who repent and trust in him, as well as to give eternal life to those who belong to him in Christ, even though God's judgment of death for sin still prevails in the present time (Rom 6:23). The promise of Christ's resurrection, and thus of our future resurrection, is assured because God keeps his promises.

God's Grace

There is bountiful evidence of God's undeserved favor expressed to humanity through the ages. This is clearly evident in the story of Esther. Neither Mordecai nor Esther is portrayed as a squeaky-clean character, either in terms of keeping the Jewish customs or in lifestyle. As Laniak insightfully comments, "Biblical narratives rarely describe their heroes without an almost embarrassing transparency regarding their shortcomings, frailties, and moral failures. ... Biblical history celebrates the deliverance of God (named or not), generally accomplished with the most unlikely partners."[3] Mordecai sparks Haman's rage by his defiance—his refusal to show honor where honor is ostensibly due—and in so doing also deliberately transgresses the Persian law, issued by the Persian king. The storyteller gives no reason for Mordecai's defiance beyond an ancient religious grudge. Further, Esther is stunningly beautiful, yet neither she nor Mordecai makes any attempt to resist her recruitment into the king's harem. She violates her Jewish faith by having a "consensual" sexual relationship with the king—at his request—as she flaunts her beauty in the king's bedroom in her "legal" one-night stand. She so impresses the king in this regard that she earns his favor and her crown. Yet in spite of her unconventional lifestyle and lack of conformity to the Jewish law and morals, she nevertheless is God's instrument. This is part of how she gets to be royalty, which later proves critical to the preservation of the Jews. Esther is thus, just like Mordecai, a trophy of God's grace.

> In spite of Esther's unconventional lifestyle and her lack of conformity to the Jewish law and morals, she is nevertheless God's instrument.

This truth transforms the Christian's life, as none of us are squeaky-clean people either. In spite of our flaws and deviance from God's prescribed ways to live a holy life, God nevertheless uses even us. And what is more, he works through our flaws so that people will see that he, not us, is the one at work.[4] God's grace at work in our lives shows forth his glory; he—not the imperfect people he uses to accomplish his purposes—receives the praise!

God's Rule

The story of Esther starts off with a highly impressive, powerful ruler over a vast empire. He is the most powerful man on the face of the earth. Yet the real King who rules the world is present invisibly in the shadows. Even though he is not seen, he rules. And he is far more powerful than anyone could ever imagine. He rules not merely one epoch of time, but for all eternity. His rule is unrivaled, and his kingdom has no end. When the curtain eventually falls at the end of time (whenever that may be), all the rulers of the earth will bow before God as the King of all kings and the Lord of all lords. Unlike the situation in the story of Daniel, the earthly king in Esther's story does not acknowledge the supremacy of the king of Mordecai and Esther (Dan 4:34–35). Jesus is the ultimate king; he is given the name above all names and the ultimate honor by his Father in heaven because of his self-sacrificial death to save the world from God's judgment (Phil 2:9–11).

This truth transforms the Christian's life because we know with certainty that God rules the world; he has done so from the beginning of time and will continue to do so until its end; thereafter he will rule for all eternity. He is a loving ruler who desires an intimate relationship with those he has created in his likeness. One coming day all people in Christ will reign together with him for ever and ever (Rev 22:3–5).

He is a loving ruler who desires an intimate relationship with those he created in his likeness.

SUGGESTED READING

- ☐ Proverbs 16:9; 19:21
- ☐ 1 Peter 2:11–12

Reflection

How has the Esther story proved that God, even though unseen, is at work in your life and in the world?

How do you feel about God using flawed people to accomplish his purposes? How does this give you hope that God may use you too?

What characteristics in your life will undeniably demonstrate that you are trusting God in your everyday life?

BIBLIOGRAPHY

Allen, Leslie C., and Timothy S. Laniak. *Ezra, Nehemiah, Esther.* Understanding the Bible Commentary Series. Grand Rapids: Baker, 2012.

Bartholomew, Craig. G., and David J. H. Beldman, eds. *Hearing the Old Testament.* Grand Rapids: Eerdmans, 2012.

Beckett, Michael. *Gospel in Esther*. Milton Keynes, UK: Paternoster Press, 2002.

Berlin, Adele. *Esther*. JPS Bible Commentary. Philadelphia: Jewish Publication Society, 2001.

Bloomfield, Peter. *The Guide: Esther.* Darlington, UK: Evangelical Press, 2002.

Bush, Frederic. *Ruth, Esther.* Word Biblical Commentary 9. Dallas: Word, 1996.

Clines, David J. A. *The Esther Scroll: The Story of the Story*, Journal of the Study of the Old Testament Supplement Series 30. Sheffield, England: JSOT Press, 1984.

Dandamayev, Muhammad A. "Courts and Courtiers i. In the Median and Achaemenid periods." In *Encyclopedia Iranica*. Winona Lake, IN: Eisenbrauns, 1982–. Article published December 15, 1993. Last modified November 2, 2011. http://www.iranicaonline.org/articles/courts-and-courtiers-i.

Duguid, Iain M. *Esther & Ruth.* Reformed Expository Commentary. Philipsburg, NJ: P&R Publishinng, 2005.

Dumbrell, William J. *The Faith of Israel: A Theological Survey of the Old Testament.* Nottingham: Apollos, 1988.

Firth, David. *The Message of Esther.* The Bible Speaks Today. Downers Grove, IL: InterVarsity Press, 2010.

Fox, Michael. V. *Character and Ideology in the Book of Esther.* Grand Rapids: Eerdmans, 1991.

Gordis, Robert. "Studies in the Esther Narrative." *Journal of Biblical Literature* 95 (1976): 43–58.

Jobes, Karen. *Esther*. NIV Application Commentary. Grand Rapids: Zondervan, 1999.

Kuhrt, Amélie. *The Ancient Near East c. 3000–330 BC.* Vol. 2. New York: Routledge, 1995.

Milne, Bruce. *Know the Truth.* Downers Grove, IL: InterVarsity Press, 1982.

Moore, Carey A. *Esther*. Anchor Bible 7B. Garden City, NY: Doubleday, 1971.

Paton, Lewis Bayles. *The Book of Esther.* International Critical Commentary. Edinburgh: T&T Clark, 1908.

Reid, Debra. *Esther: An Introduction and Commentary.* Tyndale Old Testament Commentaries 13. Downers Grove, IL: IVP Academic, 2008.

Sternberg, Meir. *The Poetics of Biblical Narrative*. Bloomington: Indiana University Press, 1987.

Tidball, Dianne. *Esther: A True First Lady.* Fearn, Milton Keynes, Scotland: Christian Focus Publications, 2001.

Tull, Patricia K. "Esther, Book of." In *The Lexham Bible Dictionary.* Edited by John D. Barry, et al. Bellingham, WA: Lexham Press, 2012–2015.

Webb, Barry. *Five Festal Garments: Christian Reflections on The Song of Songs, Ruth, Lamentations, Ecclesiastes and Esther.* New Studies in Biblical Theology. Downers Grove, IL: InterVarsity Press, 2000.

Whitcomb, Kelly A., and Trisha Wheelock. "Esther, Additions to." In *The Lexham Bible Dictionary.* Edited by John D. Barry, et al. Bellingham, WA: Lexham Press, 2012–2015.

Yamauchi, Edwin. *Persia and the Bible.* Grand Rapids: Baker, 1990.

NOTES

Chapter 1: Introduction

1. My interpretive framework for writing this book was shaped significantly by insights gleaned from these commentaries:

Allen, Leslie. C., and Laniak, Timothy S., *Ezra, Nehemiah, Esther*, Understanding the Bible Commentary Series (Grand Rapids: Baker, 2003).

Berlin, Adele, *Esther*, JPS Bible Commentary (Philadelphia: Jewish Publication Society, 2001).

Firth, David, *The Message of Esther*, The Bible Speaks Today (Downers Grove, IL: InterVarsity Press, 2010).

Jobes, Karen, *Esther*, NIV Application Commentary (Grand Rapids: Zondervan, 1999).

For further academic discussion, see my bibliography.

2. David J. A. Clines may have been the first person to apply this phrase to the book of Esther in *The Esther Scroll: The Story of the Story*, Journal of the Study of the Old Testament: Supplement Series 30 (Sheffield: JSOT Press, 1984), 36. It appears to have been commonly used by commentators since that time.

3. Susa may refer to a fortified area or the palace situated on a hill above the rest of the city. It may also refer to the larger city and surrounding area. It is sometimes unclear which is being referred to in Esther (see Esth 1:5). Sees, note on Esther 1:2.

4. The ancient Greek and Latin versions of Esther includes six major additions (in 107 verses). While the Hebrew text does not include an explicit mention of God, the Greek and Latin versions do. These additions do not appear to be original to the book of Esther. See "Esther, Additions to," in *The Lexham Bible Dictionary*, ed. John D. Barry, et al. (Bellingham, WA: Lexham Press, 2012–2015).

5. Adele Berlin, *The JPS Bible Commentary: Esther* (Philadelphia: The Jewish Publication Society, 2001), xxiii.

Chapter 2: A Portrait of Esther

1. See "Esther, Book of," in *Lexham Bible Dictionary*, ed. John D. Barry, et al. (Bellingham, WA: Lexham Press, 2012–2015).

2. Berlin, *Esther*, xlviii.

3."The most brilliant period of Persian history was that under the Achaemenid rulers—Cyrus and his successors. They extended the Persian Empire to Egypt and Turkey to the west and Bactria and the Indus Valley to the east. During this period the Persians under Darius and Xerxes were defeated by the heroic efforts of the Greeks in 490 at Marathon, in 480 at Salamis, and in 479 at Plataea and Mycale" (Edwin M. Yamauchi, *Persia and the Bible* [Grand Rapids: Baker, 1990], 23).

Chapter 3: Narrative: The Fascination of Story

1. Berlin, *Esther*, xxxii.

2. Frederic Bush, *Ruth, Esther*, Word Biblical Commentary 9 (Dallas: Word, 1996), 297.

3. The Hellenistic period begins in the late fourth century. Amélie Kuhrt, *The Ancient Near East c. 3000–330 BC*, Volume 2 (New York: Routledge, 1995), 649.

4. For more on this idea, see Karen Jobes, *Esther*, NIV Application Commentary (Grand Rapids: Zondervan, 1999), 38.

5. Meir Sternberg, *The Poetics of Biblical Narrative* (Bloomington: Indiana University Press, 1987), 90.

6. Ibid., 259–60 (italics original).

7. Jobes, *Esther*, 37.

8. Berlin, *Esther*, xvii.

9. Craig. G. Bartholomew and David J. H. Beldman, eds., *Hearing the Old Testament* (Grand Rapids: Eerdmans, 2012), 78. Beldman goes on to illustrate this using the Esther story.

10. Ibid., 79.

11.David Firth, *The Message of Esther*, The Bible Speaks Today (Downers Grove, IL: InterVarsity, 2010), 33.

12. Leslie C. Allen and Timothy S. Laniak (*Ezra, Nehemiah, Esther*, Understanding the Bible Commentary Series [Grand Rapids: Baker, 2012], 177–82) helpfully outline some of the historical problems and make a case for its historicity to be reconsidered.

13. Berlin, *Esther*, xvii.

14. Jobes, *Esther*, 37.

15. Allen and Laniak, *Ezra, Nehemiah, Esther*, 182.

16. Berlin, *Esther*, 91.

Chapter 4: Scene One: A Pretty Jew in the King's Palace

1. Also known by the name King Ahasuerus, identified as the historical Artaxerxes; Berlin argues, however, that the king in the book of Esther was not an actual historical character (Berlin, *Esther*, 5).

2. Kuhrt (*The Ancient Near East*, 670, 676) notes that Xerxes subdivided the empire during his reign to create a more efficient administration.

3. Carey A. Moore, *Esther*, The Anchor Bible (Garden City, NY: Doubleday, 1971), 4, quotes a foundation tablet found in Xerxes' palace at Persepolis confirming the extent of the Persian Empire under Xerxes.

4. Kuhrt (*The Ancient Near East*, 659) briefly details the exploitation of hostilities—even possibly from Jewish deportees—that led to the invasion of the Persian king Cyrus into Babylon.

5. Berlin, *Esther*, xxxiii: Xerxes led a major invasion into Greece in 480–479 BC and was defeated; Firth, *Message of Esther*, 54, cites Herodotus regarding Xerxes' loss in wars against the Greeks.

6. Berlin, *Esther*, 13.

7. Jobes, *Esther*, 68.

8. Kuhrt, *The Ancient Near East*, 676.

9. Berlin, *Esther*, 11.

10. Jobes, *Esther*, 78.

11.There does not appear to be any evidence concerning the irrevocable nature of the king's command in Persian law. However, Daniel 6:8 also indicates that Persian law was irreversible.

12. Berlin, *Esther*, 22.

13. Jeremiah 29 mentions God's instructions to Jewish exiles living under foreign powers outside their promised homeland.

14. God's use of Esther, despite her contravention of moral values and lack of Jewish distinctiveness, will be discussed further in the final chapter under the heading "God's Grace."

15. Berlin, *Esther*, 4, explains the feasts in greater depth.

16. While the text is never explicit about the sexual relationship of Esther and the king, there is no other reason for a young woman in this context to be brought to the king for a night (Esth 2:12–18).

17. There is a film based on Esther titled *One Night with the King*. Sadly, the producers do not stick strictly to the biblical storyline.

Chapter 5: Scene Two: A Jewish Holocaust Looms

1. Robert Gordis, "Studies in the Esther Narrative," *Journal of Biblical Literature* 95 (1976): 43–58.

2. Etymological information can be found here: www.behindthename.com

3. Berlin, *Esther*, 42.

4. Kuhrt, *The Ancient Near East*, 699: "Although the Achaemenid kings used local languages for their decrees, they also employed Aramaic as a kind of *lingua franca* and spread its use throughout the imperial territories."

Chapter 6: Scene Three: A Jewish Queen to the Rescue

1. Berlin, *Esther*, 45.

2. For more on Esther's character development, see Jobes, *Esther*, 139.

3. Lewis Bayles Paton, *The Book of Esther*, International Critical Commentary (Edinburgh: T&T Clark, 1908), 190, notes the irony that this is how King Xerxes' life ended. See also Kuhrt, *The Ancient Near East*, 671.

4. Garments of mourning are inappropriate in the king's palace and precincts (Esth 4:2).

Chapter 7: Scene Four: A Jew Honored by His Archenemy

1. Note the storyteller's subtle change in the order of the names from Esther 5:10 to 5:14.

2. Jobes, *Esther*, 152.

3. Kuhrt, *The Ancient Near East*, 688.

4. Jobes, *Esther*, 159.

Chapter 8: Scene Five: A Dead End for the Jews' Enemy

1. Michael V. Fox, *Character and Ideology in the Book of Esther* (Grand Rapids: Eerdmans, 1991), 86.

2. *Encyclopedia Iranica*, s.v. "Courts and Courtiers in the Median and Achaemenid period," accessed April 19, 2016, http://www.iranicaonline.org/articles/courts-and-courtiers-i

3. Kuhrt, *The Ancient Near East*, 689.

Chapter 9: Scene Six: A Royal Edict Saves the Jews

1. Berlin, *Esther*, 77.

2. This is similar both to Joseph's experience in Genesis 41:42 and to Daniel's in Daniel 5:29.

3. Berlin, *Esther*, 81.

4. Ibid., 85.

5. Joshua 11:23 refers to God giving the Israelites rest from the enemies they have conquered.

6. This is what the giving of gifts at Christmas is intended to symbolize, but we have tragically commercialized this activity beyond recognition, with the result that we tend to neglect God's gift in Jesus and shift the focus onto our Christmas gifts.

7. Fox, *Character and Ideology*, 118.

8. Berlin expresses her opinion that this ending is a literary device—literary fiction—and that the author is concluding the story: "Its loose ends have been tied up, and that it is valid—that the story is of great consequence to the reader" (*Esther*, 94).

Chapter 10: Conclusion

1. Barry Webb, *Five Festal Garments: Christian Reflections on The Song of Songs, Ruth, Lamentations, Ecclesiastes and Esther*, New Studies in Biblical Theology (Downers Grove, IL: InterVarsity, 2000), 124.

2. Bruce Milne, *Know the Truth* (Downers Grove, IL: InterVarsity, 1982), 88.

3. Allen and Laniak, *Ezra, Nehemiah, Esther*, 183.

4. Jobes notes, "[T]he Bible story from Genesis to Revelation is the story of God's reconciling fallen humanity to himself in Jesus Christ. Other than Jesus himself, the people in the biblical stories are no paragons of virtue. Each of them has serious character flaws and questionable motives." (*Esther*, 140). For this reason, Jesus alone is to be our role model.